Kim,

    I hope you enjoy this <u>true</u> story of

what is possibly right here in Pittsburgh!

     cheers,

REFOUNDER

HOW TRANSFORMATIONAL LEADERS TAKE
WHAT'S BROKEN AND MAKE IT BETTER

PATRICK COLLETTI

Be bold, don't fold, grow mold, or just be told. Country or town, lost or found, opportunities abound, let's go refound.

ISBN 13: 978-1-954020-02-3

Library of Congress Cataloging-in-Publication Data
Names: Colletti, Patrick, author.
Title: Refounder / Patrick Colletti
Description: First Edition | Texas: Per Capita Publishing (2021)
Identifiers: LCCN 2021902322 (print)

Printed in the United States of America on acid-free paper.

10 9 8 7 6 5 4 3 2 1

First Edition

To my dearest Jennifer, Hudson, and Andrew:
may you adventure, learn, play, and serve for
as long as you live.

TABLE OF CONTENTS

INTRODUCTION

In early 2020, the world came grinding to a halt. A pandemic virus was spreading across the globe, and it had made landfall on United States soil. On March 3, New York governor Andrew Cuomo announced the first person-to-person spread of COVID-19 in the Empire State. By March 13, 2020, only ten days later, the daily infection count had risen to almost 200, and medical professionals could see the writing on the wall. New York was on the verge of an uncontrollable outbreak, and the human impact would be devastating.

Caryl Russo was at the tip of the spear. A senior vice president of Robert Wood Johnson (RWJ) Barnabas Health, Caryl oversaw the occupational health needs for the workforce in the region. In collaboration with leaders across the enterprise, it was her job to ensure the healthcare system wasn't overtaxed, that it didn't fall apart because of the lack of healthy personnel or a shortage of properly fitted personal protective equipment, also known as PPE. She was responsible for ensuring that healthcare workers in her system didn't transmit the virus to otherwise healthy patients or, worse yet, become superspreaders. By mid-March, Caryl was fighting a round-the-clock battle.

Within days of the pandemic siege, healthcare providers in the region were burning through their supply of N95 masks, which seal around the mouth and nose and are designed to effectively filter particulates carrying the coronavirus. The United States Centers for Disease Control required medical personnel to discard their masks after tending to each COVID-infected patient, and with the daily uptick in new cases, the supply was running thin. Although the CDC relented within a few days, changing the policy to allow hospitals to use N95 masks for an entire day or until visibly damaged, the stockpiles had already been drained. Hospitals across New York and New Jersey scrambled for new supplies, which were critically short.

Production and distribution kicked into high gear, but masks only trickled in. N95 masks are sized to fit, though, and without the proper fit, the masks wouldn't seal and could not keep the user protected. Without the proper seal, particulates carrying the virus could sneak in around the edges, increasing the risk of infection to the healthcare workers treating COVID-19 patients. And if the healthcare workers were infected, they could transmit the disease to other coworkers, non-COVID patients, and their friends and family. If Russo couldn't secure enough supplies of correctly sized masks, the frontline workers were at risk. But with the influx of new workers and N95 masks of varying sizes, how could Russo track what mask size each new worker needed? What's more, how could facility leaders track mask supplies to ensure they had enough for the potentially long battle with COVID?

To make matters worse, with the new supplies of N95 masks, each worker was required to be refitted to ensure they received the right size, and the refitting process was not simple. Each doctor, nurse, and technician was required to take a break from their duties at a time when every break might cost lives. They'd attend a fitting, where they'd don a new mask and be spritzed with a saccharine solution. If they could taste the sweet solution, that meant the mask didn't fit and they'd need to repeat the test with a different sized mask. With thousands of employees being fitted and refitted, the testing solution ran out in some locations. Still other locations had more than enough.

As the virus shifted from community to community, Russo needed a way to track available masks, the saccharine solution, and the personnel needed to administer mask tests. If she could, she'd be able to transfer supply and personnel to the hardest hit places.

But as if the mask and PPE difficulties weren't enough, personnel shortages set in. The caseload threatened to overwhelm existing staff, and to make matters worse, some healthcare workers came down with the virus. Russo and her team put the call out for additional personnel, and the medical community responded. But how could Russo ensure that these new and existing workers (35,000 individuals spread out across 13 affiliates) hadn't traveled to COVID hotspots around the world in the days just before the pandemic hit New York? There were other employee concerns, too. If an employee was exposed to the coronavirus, how could she track quarantine times and testing results to ensure the worker was cleared to return to work? How could they screen those who might be asymptomatic carriers, who might inadvertently transfer the disease to an uninfected patient who was in the hospital for a different issue? More complicated still, how could they ensure that employees with underlying medical risks—conditions that might make COVID infection life-threatening—weren't placed on COVID wards where they might be exposed to the deadly virus?

It was crisis management on the fly, and Russo needed real-time access to exposure notifications, travel histories, PPE needs, inventory supplies, employee temperatures, and potential vectors of transmission. And this mountain of data needed to be monitored by more than just Russo. It needed to be accessed by administrators at various hospitals across the region. Once they had the data, they needed to be able to modify it on the fly to make sure everything was up to date in real time. It was too much. Absolute insanity. (Those were her words, not mine.)

Russo had called to thank me for the work our company, Net Health, had done to provide software and support. RWJ used our occupational and employee health system to track all the data and ensure that healthy, well-prepared caregivers were on the scene so that their workforce didn't become super-spreaders. Perhaps most importantly, with our software, Russo was able to keep track of N95 mask supplies and refitting solutions and was able to shift resources as needed.

"There is no doubt this saved lives," she said. "An analog solution would have been useless against this kind of pandemic. Your system was connected, easy to understand, and agile. Thank you."

We'd played a role in the war on the pandemic, and Russo wanted me to know. Before our goodbyes, she told me she felt her team represented the heroes no one saw coming. We were a part of that team, she said.

As I hung up the phone, I stepped off my front porch and onto the grass. I took a deep breath, considering how this story might have turned out differently. If we hadn't put the time, effort, and energy into refounding a tiny company—one on life-support, no less—how many lives might have been lost?

+++

Ours is a refounding story, a story of a group of people who took a broken company and built something better. How did we do it? That's what this book is about. But it's not just our story. In this book you'll meet one of the world's top innovators and one of the country's most agile educators. You'll meet an incredible community organizer who is taking back city blocks and a reporter who, despite having an average viewership of 2.5 million, switched gears for purpose-oriented entrepreneurship. You'll meet healthcare professionals who are in the business of saving limbs and lives. What do they have in common? When they came face-to-face with the brokenness of their own world, they didn't run away. Instead, they took a sober look at the world around them, focused their efforts, imagined new possibilities, and worked to create a better world for the people in their organizations or communities. They refounded their respective industries, neighborhoods, and even their lives.

It seems we come face-to-face with more brokenness by the day: the failure of politics, of communities, of corporations, of leaders. But what if the brokenness of our systems—whether corporate or otherwise—is an invitation to pause, reflect, and ask a simple question: Is there something here worth refounding?

Through the stories of the Refounders throughout this book, we'll begin to work toward a fresh approach with a new mentality, one that allows us to rebuild with practical steps when the systems of the world around us fall apart. In that rebuilding, we'll begin to see a simple truth. What's broken can be made better if we're committed to becoming Refounders.

ONE

THE REPOSSESSION

In 1999, I joined a start-up tech company with big dreams and no plans to achieve them. I was only a year out of college, part of the young, energetic, and hungry talent that had been hired to take the company from start-up to a viable health-tech company. We had investors. We had an office. We knew the tech space and could speak the lingo. There was only one problem: we didn't have a product—not really.

Unconcerned, we believed we'd be the ones to figure out a way to apply new tech to the healthcare industry. But all those dreams went up in smoke in September 2001. Just four days after the terrorist events that rocked the country, I found myself on the *business end of a call* with the new chairman of the board. There was no good way to break the news, he said, but the company was burning. As a tech company with no clear customer base and with a group of investors skittish about the potential liquidity crisis in the wake of the 9/11 attacks on

New York, we were in trouble. Without prospects of return, the shareholders were out of cash to inject. There was debt to cover, too, though he couldn't say exactly how much. A few board members were willing to cover a reduced payroll for only two employees—our CMU software developer Chris Hayes and me—and even then, we'd only have three months to turn the company around.

"We'll understand if you walk away, but we'll give you a couple of months to try and turn it around."

The cascade of bad news washed over me. I froze.

"Patrick?"

The voice on the other side of the line pulled me back into the moment.

"You heard me, right?"

Three months to restart a company, mountains of debt, and no cash. Was it possible? My heart pounded in my throat and my mind raced.

"Patrick?"

"Let me talk to Jen and get back with you," I said. But I already knew the answer. We'd made too many promises to too many people. We couldn't afford to be wrong.

I slipped the phone in my pocket and stood in the tiny living room of our first apartment. Staring out the window, I considered my next call. I had to tell her, though it would be no surprise. Jen had known this was a risky endeavor, that it didn't have much financial runway left. In fact, she knew it was risky when she agreed to marry me, but had she known the company was in the middle of a collapse? Truth be told, I hadn't known it. She'd be shocked, and so would her parents. And once the cat was out of the bag, I'd have some explaining to do. My father-in-law, Gene, had read the tea leaves from the beginning.

In the spring of 2000, I'd driven to Hudson, Ohio, a leafy suburb of Cleveland, to have breakfast with Jen's parents. That weekend, Jen and I were headed to Denver, where she spent the first sixteen years of her life. I hoped to propose to her in her childhood hometown, but I wanted to get her father's blessing first. So, I dropped in unannounced for what appeared to be an impromptu breakfast (even though it wasn't so impromptu). Ring in my pocket, I made small talk and fought nerves as I meandered toward the point.

Fidgeting with the box in my pocket, drumming up the nerve to ask for the family blessing, Gene ambushed my line of attack. Jen told him I'd left my relatively stable career and joined an upstart tech company in the heart of Pittsburgh. Pittsburgh, a blue-collar steel town, was in its early days of unproven tech expansion, not the most likely place for a breakout tech company, and Gene said as much before leveling his questions. What were the company's prospects? And what exactly did the company do?

It was stable, I said. It would keep us off the streets (and out of his basement), I promised. There was nothing but upside, I said, and I believed it. Jen's mother listened and offered more juice and toast with a very unconvinced look on her face. Jen's dad offered more questions. I answered him as best as I could, then turned the conversation to his daughter. I wanted his blessing to marry her, and though I suspect he had his reservations based on the breakfast inquisition, he agreed, perhaps thinking our marriage was (more or less) a fait accompli.

That was only a year earlier, and now, here I was, swimming in the news of failure just days after a national tragedy. As I walked to the car, I could feel the churning in my stomach. I second-guessed everything, considered my old career path in legal media and advertising and how much more stable it was. Lawyers always seemed to come out on the high side of any recession and always had money to burn.

Over the weekend and into the next week, I ran the pros and cons with Jen and Chris. By the following Thursday, we'd all come to the same conclusion. Chris and I would stay on and see this through to the end. We'd do our best to capitalize on the company's noble ambition—to make a difference in healthcare—or we'd go down trying. If we succeeded, we'd be a comeback story, and what person hasn't dreamed of coming back against all odds?

The following Friday, over a coffee in the William Penn hotel, Chris and I asked ourselves what would need to be true in order to get back on track. Sure, we'd need to slash debt. Yes, we'd need to figure out how to grow revenue, but how? We weren't sure, so we created a sort of task-by-task Refounders playbook that might give us a fighting chance to turn this company around. We typed the task list on our laptops.

TASK 1: DETERMINE HOW MUCH MONEY WE OWED AND TO WHOM

What should have been the easiest task grew more complicated when we discovered hundreds of unopened bills at the office on the Monday after my phone call with the chairman of the board. There were bills from accountants, lawyers, and copier services. There were bills from a furniture rental company and one from the landlord. Even Einstein's Bagels sent a collection notice for an outstanding account of less than $100. It would take days to open the bills, to log them, review them, and sort out how much we could pay. It might take an army of bookkeepers to straighten it all out, but we couldn't afford to retain one. We'd have to do it ourselves, and we were neither an army nor were we bookkeepers.

TASK 2: FACE THE DEBT HOLDERS AND CONVINCE THEM TO NOT FORCE US INTO BANKRUPTCY

After slashing payroll and cutting every non-essential expense, we'd still be bleeding cash. We'd have to go hat-in-hand to our creditors—accountants, lawyers, and even the manager at Einstein's Bagels. If they wouldn't take pennies on the dollar, if they wouldn't restructure our debt, we were dead in the water. We'd be forced into involuntary bankruptcy.

TASK 3: COMMUNICATE WITH THE SHAREHOLDERS

The shareholders—did they know the details? It was unclear in those early days, but if the company was to survive, we'd need their buy-in. They'd invested in the vision, uncertain as it was. If we were going to make it, we'd need their support, their buy-in, their cash, and their commitment to the turn-around. And if we couldn't gain their trust through open and honest communication, we'd never survive.

TASK 4: PICK A LANE AND CUT THE FAT

We were a three-product idea company, though none of those products were all that compelling. We needed a single concept, something salable, and we needed to go all in. Like extraneous expenses, the side-projects and fallback ideas had to be cut. Creating a viable company required focus, even if we didn't yet know exactly where to focus.

TASK 5: FIND CUSTOMERS

A product without customers won't create a viable company. Chris and I weren't geniuses, but we knew that much. We needed a product, one that met a need in the market and generated customers. How would we do it? We didn't know.

TASK 6: CONVINCE THE BOARD

The board had trusted a handful of energetic boneheads to run a company, and we'd failed. As a result, we'd spent what relational capital we had. We had a month to pull together a viable plan, one that would bolster their confidence in us. Then, two more months to execute. And though it might be a difficult sell, we believed we could do it. After all, they'd already had enough confidence to give us a few months.

If we followed the playbook, if we ran the tasks, would we succeed? We weren't sure, but it was worth a shot. We were in Pittsburgh, and Pittsburgh is a city that never quits.

PITTSBURGH: A CITY OF REFOUNDERS

Pittsburgh has a folkloric reputation. It's a town built on the backs of stout immigrants, people who embody the enterprising spirit of America and have a never-say-die attitude. And having lived in Pittsburgh for the entirety of my adult life, I know the truth of this story. It's a Refounder's story that spans over two centuries.

In its earliest days, the British controlled the Point, a triangular section of land that juts out into the three rivers that come together here: the Allegheny, the Monongahela, and the Ohio. But in 1754, during the French and Indian War, an invading French army demanded British surrender of the Point and erected Fort Duquesne. Four years later, a young George Washington guided General John Forbes and a British army back to the Point, where they forced a French retreat. Forbes named the tiny settlement around Fort Duquesne "Pittsburgh," pronounced "Pitts-boro," like Edinburgh, Scotland. Later, the British would rebuild the fort, naming it Fort Pitt.

It was an early port town, a gateway to the western frontier. It was a region rich in natural resources, having access to deep veins of coal, natural gas, iron, and limestone. Timber was also plentiful, and so, the city became a hub of commerce in the days running up to the American Revolution. During the days of the Revolution, Pittsburgh became the original gateway to the American West, and Fort Pitt housed revolutionary troops.

From the beginning, the people of Pittsburgh have been Refounders and revolutionaries. They've nursed a rebellious streak, too. A town which loved its liquor as much as its work, Pittsburghers kicked off the Whiskey Rebellion of 1794 when the young American government imposed steep taxes on small distillers. The rebels fended off the new regressive tax for several years, but the rebellion came to a head when small farmers from the surrounding community were met by a federal militia amassed by then-President George Washington.

He rode at the head of a 13,000-member army made up of militiamen from neighboring states, and together, they quelled the rebellion. It's the only time in American history that a sitting president led the military in the field. And though the conflict was resolved without violence, the people of the city sent a clear message: The people of Pittsburgh would not silently tolerate what they viewed as injustice.

The spit-fire spirit of the people of Pittsburgh has always been its advantage. As a hub of iron and arms, the city thrived during the Civil War. Shortly after, Pittsburgh citizens like Andrew Carnegie—a railroad bridge-builder and Scottish immigrant—took advantage of every opportunity. A born innovator, Carnegie parlayed early business earnings into a foothold in the steel industry, investing in the new Bessemer steelmaking process. The investment in innovation would lead to the creation of Carnegie Steel (now U.S. Steel). And through continued innovations and refinements in the steel-making process, Carnegie's steel empire enriched the people of Pittsburgh and made him the second wealthiest American in history. Some even report that at the height of his wealth, he had an inflation-adjusted net worth of $309 billion,[1] which is more than Bill Gates and Jeff Bezos combined.

Carnegie's spirit of innovation was contagious. In 1871, at the age of only twenty-one, Henry Clay Frick formed a partnership, the Frick Coke Company, with two of his cousins. Using beehive ovens, they turned coal to coke, an element needed by Carnegie and others to manufacture steel. In fact, Frick's process was so integral to the steel-making process that

---

1. Gus Lubin, "The 13 Richest Americans of All Time," *Business Insider* (April 17, 2011), https://www.businessinsider.com/richest-americans-ever-2011-4.

Carnegie exchanged a portion of his interest in Carnegie Steel for an interest in the Frick Coke Company.

The city of Pittsburgh—a city of innovation—was built on coal and steel, but the enterprising spirit was infectious. H. J. Heinz, one of the first mass producers of tomato ketchup, pioneered efforts in food safety in manufacturing. He was a generous man, too, one who cared about corporate culture before caring about corporate culture was cool. He provided his employees with medical care, recreational facilities, and educational opportunities. It was an innovative approach in an age where so many captains of industry seemed to care little for their employees.

Over the years, the city has given birth to more than its fair share of innovators: Andrew Mellon, an early investment banker and politician whose name comprises half of Carnegie Mellon University; Andy Warhol, a Pittsburgh-born artist who pioneered his silk-screening process; Fred Rogers, whose *Mr. Rogers' Neighborhood* revolutionized early childhood television; Rachel Carson, who developed her appreciation of the natural world in Pittsburgh and ultimately challenged the practices of agricultural scientists by exposing the hazards of the pesticide DDT, calling for a change in the way humankind viewed its relationship with the natural world; Dr. Thomas Starzl, whose pioneering work in organ preservation, anti-rejection treatments, and transplant has been cited more than any other researcher in the world; and Jonas Salk, the virologist and professor at the University of Pittsburgh who developed the polio vaccine. This revolutionary, innovative, refounding spirit helped the city thrive throughout the mid-twentieth century. But in the decades leading up to the turn of the millennium, everything changed.

By the mid-1900s, Pittsburgh accounted for nearly half of the nation's steel production. But in 1980, the United States economy was hard hit, and Pittsburgh entered a deep depression. Consumer demand for steel products waned, the price plummeted, and the steel markets dried up almost overnight. The backbone of the city's economy was broken, and more than 150,000 steel workers were laid off. Steel mills closed.[2] Companies supporting the steel industry suffered. And despite the Steelers winning four Super Bowls in just six years and the Pirates winning two World Series in the same decade, the city had little else to celebrate. The Pittsburgh metro area unemployment rate topped out at 18.2 percent, significantly higher than the national employment rate of 10.5 percent.[3]

Of the city's twentieth-century depression, Marlee Myers, a member of Pittsburgh's now-thriving business community, said, "This region had been dependent on the steel industry and the many jobs it provided and we were really at a crossroads. [Pittsburgh] could have gone the direction of other failing Rust Belt cities, or we could reinvent ourselves."[4] And so, Pittsburgh did what it always had; it reinvented itself, refounded, innovated. How? We'll examine it more in the pages of this book, but for now, know this: its crowning qualities—hard-working people, a spirit of innovation, and a

---

2. Daniel Rowe, "Lessons from the Steel Crisis of the 1980s," *The Conversation* (April 15, 2016), https://theconversation.com/lessons-from-the-steel-crisis-of-the-1980s-57751.

3. Christopher Briem, "Recessions and Pittsburgh," *Pittsburgh Economic Quarterly* (December 2008), https://ucsur.pitt.edu/files/peq/peq_2008-12.pdf.

4. Worth watching: a friend and CEO of the Pittsburgh Technology Council sums up the shift (November 5, 2012), https://www.bing.com/videos/search?q=pittsburgh+pivot+video&view=detail&mid=EE19CE8BE106A061D6EEEE19CE-8BE106A061D6EE&FORM=VIRE.

never-say-die attitude—have transformed it from a smoky steel city to something more modern. It reimagined possibilities and turned to robotics, artificial intelligence, healthcare tech, advanced manufacturing, and autonomous mobility.

The people of Pittsburgh are Refounders. Whether forts, industrial processes, industries, or districts in our city, refounding is in our DNA. Maybe this is what drove Chris and me to take on the reclamation project that would become Net Health. Maybe we'd been inspired by the spirit of Pittsburgh.

FOUNDER OR REFOUNDER?

The Net Health story serves as a sort of microcosm of Pittsburgh. When the chips were down, the team refocused, reimagined possibilities, and refounded the company. We refused to quit (like Washington), identified market niches (like Carnegie and Frick), and invested in corporate culture (like Heinz). The result? The company's software serves 96 percent of the nation's largest health systems and facilitates the healing of millions of patients each year.

If it were just the numbers we cared about, we'd be justified in calling the results a success. Even more amazing, though, Net Health has become a place of purpose, one which found its way by creating software solutions geared toward "Reuniting caregivers with their calling" (our corporate slogan). Together, the team has solved some of the largest and most poorly understood problems in healthcare. What's more, we've created an amazing culture, and our employees look forward to making a difference through their contribution.

We built a successful company and amazing corporate

culture with a Refounder's ethos. But what is a Refounder? For comparison and contrast, it may be helpful to juxtapose Refounders with the modern darling of Silicon Valley founders.

Founders start with little more than a raw idea and the willpower to see it to life. The moniker might bring to mind Tesla's Elon Musk. Founders go all-in on an idea, hoping to create something from nothing. And the truth is, the world has benefited greatly from its founders.

Refounders share the same gene as founders, though it's expressed in different ways. Like founders, they are visionaries, but they take a different approach. They are the turnaround artists, the men and women who reimagine existing but broken structures and aim to improve them. They are magicians, taking the raw materials of a company, culture, or even a life, and transforming them into something more meaningful. Put more simply, Refounders use their magic to create something better from something broken.

In an article for the *Harvard Business Review*, "CEOs Should Think Like Founders, Not Just Managers," David Kidder and John Geraci shared the mindset of successful CEOs. Chief executives, they argued, are not simply managing the day-to-day affairs. Instead, they think like Refounders. But what is a Refounder precisely? According to Kidder and Geraci, "Refounders are leaders who, despite not having started the company, think with the mindset of a founder. They . . . look to leverage their company's assets to build new offerings, move into new markets, and create next-generation solutions."[5]

---

5. David Kidder and John Garaci, "CEOs Should Think Like Founders, Not Just Managers," *Harvard Business Review* (November 13, 2017), https://hbr.org/2017/11/ceos-should-think-like-founders-not-just-managers.

In other words, Refounders are not content to manage the status quo. Instead, they focus on repairing, renewing, renovating, and ultimately cultivating something better.

The world needs founders. It needs start-ups. But founders and start-ups are not enough. Refounders are critical to a world that's constantly in flux. Innovation, changing social structures, and even pandemic concerns—like those we experienced in the COVID-19 outbreak—threaten our existing companies, educational systems, and communities. And if those institutions are to survive these changes, it will take people with a Refounder's mentality to create something better from something broken. Refounders—we are society's hedge against entropy.

I've had more than two decades to consider our crossroads moment, the moment when Chris and I (and a group of committed shareholders) made the decision to be Refounders. I've heard the stories of others who've found themselves in similar places, too, and I've come to a simple conclusion: We often miss great opportunities in the easy times. Sometimes the best opportunities arise during a moment of crisis. It might present as a giant burden, a broken relationship, or a corporate hot mess. But it's those moments that can trigger a great refounding moment if we'll let them. And if we're going to act in those moments, we must be prepared. We must develop different ways of thinking and acting. That's precisely what this book is about.

In this book, I'll lead you through the process of developing a Refounder's mentality. I'll show you how we took a certifiable dumpster fire and turned it into what my friend Mary calls "a billion-dollar company with heart." Even more, I'll show you how our refounding led to the creation of a community with purpose, one that brings life to its people and the world around it. I'll also share the stories of those who've applied some of these same refounding principles to grow successful and thriving organizations and to bring meaningful change to the world around them. Through these stories, we'll see just how a Refounder's attitude paves the way for amazing outcomes.

What's more, we'll map how the Refounders take a similar method to every problem they tackle. What is the Refounder's approach? I'll paraphrase it in step-by-step fashion:

Step 1: Refounders aren't afraid to take a sober look at hard realities.

Step 2: Identifying what's broken, Refounders selectively focus.

Step 3: Refounders imagine audacious/bold new possibilities, even if those possibilities seem remote.

Step 4: Refounders spring to action, creating better realities for people, both those in their immediate communities and in the world at large.

As you read, internalize this Refounder's approach. Memorize it. Notice how it shapes the Refounder's way of being.

Chances are, you're in a position to be a Refounder. Some area in your life—your company, community, or even your marriage—might be broken. Perhaps you haven't taken the time to stop, take a sober look, and kill the noise long enough to imagine new possibilities, and then work toward creating better realities for the people around you. If that's you, then this is your invitation to develop the Refounder's edge. Are you ready to take something that's broken and make something better? If so, come along.

REFOUNDER TAKEAWAYS

- Refounders share the same gene as founders, though it's expressed in different ways.
- Refounders focus on repairing, renewing, renovating, and ultimately cultivating something better.
- Refounders take a sober look, identify what's broken, imagine new possibilities, and work to create better realities for others.

TWO

REIMAGINING WHAT'S POSSIBLE

Our early corporate struggles were emblematic of so much that is wrong in the healthcare industry. We had bloated budgets and bled cash on overvalued resources. We poured time and energy into the wrong products and explored too many far-fetched opportunities rather than proving we could make a difference in the areas of our expertise. We were more focused on striking gold than producing software for caregivers who were providing meaningful care to patients, which is to say nothing about our care for the employees. The result? We were a certifiable, unmitigated, raging dumpster fire of a company.

Days after solidifying our draft Refounders playbook, I was on the phone with another vendor repeating the same spiel I'd run a dozen times that day. Yes, they'd provided the service. Yes, we owed the money. Yes, we were embarrassed about the situation, and no, we didn't have the cash. Could we settle the debt for a few pennies on the dollar? A long pause that followed (there was always a long pause), and the woman on the other end of the line asked me to hold. That's when two men with a dolly came through the front door.

The shorter, stockier man came my way, handed me a card, then turned and took charge like he owned the place. They were from the office furniture company, at least, that's what the card indicated. They'd come to repossess their belongings. This is, evidently, what happens when you don't pay off financed office equipment.

I waved to get Chris's attention, but he was on the far side of the room, pacing. He was on the phone with his mother, fending off her questions. Everything was fine, he said. There was a plan, he said. This was true in a sense: that is, if allowing two twenty-somethings to attempt a corporate resurrection for a company with no real product constitutes a plan. As he paced, he made space for the movers, who were carting off what used to be his desk.

The hold music was interrupted by someone who identified herself as a manager. Her voice was cold, matter-of-fact. She couldn't negotiate the debt, she said. It was above her pay-grade. Someone else would be in touch in the next few days, she said, which sounded like some vague threat. I thanked her, hung up the phone, and watched the disassembly of the office. I needed to call the chairman of the board, a relatively new member with a background in running very large healthcare organizations and who had recently managed several corporate turnarounds. He'd need an update, but I'd wait till the end of the day. I needed some space to breathe, to think.

Staring out the window, I recalled my first job, the job

I'd left almost two years earlier. I had a spacious office in One Oxford Centre, the 45-floor shiny tower downtown for a private equity-backed legal media company. I was a young, brash, suit-wearing salesman with an office overlooking downtown Pittsburgh. I rolled with executives and attorneys who wore Ferragamo wingtips and suits that cost more than my car. I made calls on clients—law firms and lawyers—throughout Pennsylvania. I was mesmerized by all the mahogany in all those offices. My boss, Harry, was a fantastic human. My salary was good for my age. The perks—great healthcare, incentive compensation, travel to unique events, paid time off—were better than I hoped. It was the kind of job that should have excited me.

I'd made contributions at the company. I'd collaborated with our new CEO—who was fresh off a stint as a senior executive at the *New York Times*—to identify an acquisition target, a local media company in Pittsburgh that would help us expand our footprint. And aside from the fact that when the initial meeting took place I had to pick up our three top executives in the used two-door car my mother gave me as a college graduation gift, I was pretty excited. I was going places.

Still, it didn't take long for the honeymoon to wear off. The culture was built on misaligned incentives. Many felt they had to fend for themselves. Internal teams didn't collaborate well, and they weren't oriented toward a common goal. Values were mismatched throughout different departments. Some focused on commissions, others on journalistic integrity, and others still on rapid growth. Departments seemed pitted against one another.

I spoke with my friends across the corporate world, and

their experiences were similar. Their managers focused on the politics of business more than the underlying fundamentals. Sarcasm and cynicism were the defaults. Was this just the way it was? The jockeying for position? The wrangling to get to the top of the corporate ladder? The profits-over-people hustle?

I may have had the skills to succeed but envisioned my future twenty years down the road. Was this what I wanted? Hardly. Only one year in and I knew that though I was getting some good experience, I had to make a change. Still, I'd wait for the right opportunity. And within a few months, it had come knocking.

A friend who ran an early tech start-up was looking for a consultant. He called me. Why? I suppose I dressed the part of a successful businessman. After all, I could speak the language of tech. I was comfortable distilling abstract ideas and putting language around those ideas, a skill that was lacking in his company. What's more, he offered more than a fair price for my services. So, I agreed to the consulting gig and began moonlighting with the company we would later rename Net Health.

Months into my consultancy, that friend approached me with an offer. They were raising money and could offer me a full-time role with significant responsibilities, he said. It was an opportunity to get in at the ground floor, and if everything went well, it could pay off. It was risky, that much was true, but when I ran the opportunity by my then-girlfriend Jen, she supported the change and the challenge. Still, she was a little confused about what exactly the company did. Truth be told, so was I. But, fascinated by the prospect, I jumped.

Those early days were golden. In fact, I thought the

opportunity was everything I wanted. It was a laid-back atmosphere, one in which most of my teammates wore flip-flops and T-shirts. (For the record, I continued to wear my suit and tie; after all, someone had to be the professional.) We celebrated creativity and stomped on stuffiness. We worked together in teams, explored any idea in healthcare disruption that might solidify our position in the space. Chris—a college intern who rolled into work mid-morning, sometimes hungover from the night before—was a unique collaborator. He was a sort of social intellectual who was bright enough to attend Carnegie Mellon University. He was the president of his fraternity and a dedicated soccer player. He could work circles around his peers.

When we weren't pursuing one of our numerous product ideas, we'd imagine new possibilities. Sometimes, Dr. Lewis Mehl-Madrona, a product collaborator and natural medicine practitioner who promoted the concept of "Coyote Medicine," invited us into his Native American healing seminars, which were sometimes accompanied by drum circles. This was creativity, man. It was the Big Lebowski talking healthcare tech at a Rusted Root concert, and we were into it. And eventually, all this creativity would pay off.

At least, that's what I'd told myself.

Seventeen months after joining, the only drum I heard was the dull thud of a hammer while the workers disassembled the cubicles—and perhaps the pounding headache this mess created. I was standing in a near-vacant office. We owned little more than a desk, some old chairs, a table, and the weight of our failure. These and our imaginations would be our only refounding assets. And as we learned, imagination can be a powerful tool.

AUDACIOUS IMAGINATION

In the second decade of the twenty-first century, downtown Pittsburgh became a sort of midwestern Silicon Valley, a tech hub in a colder, steelier town. I'll share more details in the coming chapters, but as Pittsburgh took great strides in refounding its future around technology, it found itself a hub for an aggressive, innovative, and commercially desirable technology: robotics, advanced manufacturing, and driver-less cars.

On an average winter day, I can walk from the office to the great array of shops and restaurants in the Strip District, and at some point along the way, I'll see a car making the rounds with some advanced and sleek monitoring device on the roof. The car could be operated by any number of com-panies—Aptiv, Argo AI, Aurora, Uber—each of which have facilities within blocks of the office.

You'd think I'd get used to seeing autonomous vehicles making the way through the Strip District, but each time, I smile. These cars represent the sci-fi dreams of my generation, a world in which artificial intelligence automates anything that might improve the quality of life. And only a handful of years ago, I would have imagined the idea of a fleet of automated vehicles as next to impossible. Now, I'm a believer.

Like many people, I've taken a keen interest in autono-mous cars and extreme innovation, and this interest has led me down a bit of a rabbit hole. I've researched the companies who've gone all-in on innovative technology. I've researched the people behind the projects, too. One of the most interest-ing among them is Astro Teller.

Astro and I first met as fellow tech leaders of a small

company. We worked a block away from each other and had some common investors. We shared frustrations with the gap between great ideas and getting other people to take action on these plans. But it wasn't just his extraordinary background and résumé that made him special. He was engaging and open, intense, yet interesting enough to invite free discussion. At the time he was working on a product that would monitor vital signs and "learn," based on your movement. It was something like a Whoop band, Oura ring, or Fitbit, but it was about fifteen years ahead of any of those products. He fit the role of tech entrepreneur, too—he had long hair and had already written a science fiction novel entitled *Exegesis*. He was the real deal.

Eric "Astro" Teller is that rare sort of person, the kind who inspires both belief and awe. His grandfather on his mother's side was Gerard Debreu, a Nobel Prize–winning economist. His paternal grandfather was theoretical physicist Edward Teller, who is often called the "father of the hydrogen bomb." Teller may have hit the genetic jackpot as far as genius goes, and he hasn't wasted a single neuron. He attended Stanford University, where he earned his bachelor's of science in computer science and his master's of science in symbolic computation. He went on to obtain a doctorate in artificial intelligence at Pittsburgh's Carnegie Mellon University. He is a self-described entrepreneur, scientist, inventor, author, and intelligent technological expert.

In 2010, after starting several companies, Teller joined Google X—now known simply as X—which, describes itself as "The Moonshot Factory." On its website, the company states:

X is a diverse group of inventors and entre-
preneurs who build and launch technologies
that aim to improve the lives of millions, even
billions, of people. Our goal: 10x impact on
the world's most intractable problems, not
just 10% improvement. We approach projects that have the aspiration and riskiness of
research with the speed and ambition of a
startup.

What does this mean? It may seem a little murky until
you look at a handful of X projects, each with its own cryptic,
one-word codename.

Through a project called Loon, Teller set out to cure a
simple problem: Billions of people in the world were without
access to the internet and were "completely left out of a digital revolution that could improve their finances, education,
and health." Recognizing the impossibility of creating an
infrastructure capable of delivering internet access from the
ground up, the Loon team asked how they deliver it from the
sky down. The result of their outside-the-box theory? X built
a stratospheric network of balloons traveling at the edge of
space, beaming internet connectivity down to rural areas.[6]
While recently shuttered, the program was a success, and
as of the writing of this book, Loon has delivered services
in Kenya and rural Peru and the Amazon. What's more,
it delivered emergency connectivity in Puerto Rico after
Hurricane Maria in 2017. By imagining possibilities, Loon

---

6. As of the writing of this book, Loon has served customers in Peru, Haiti, and
Kenya. See https://www.x.company/projects/loon/.

delivered on its core promise.

Wing was the company's attempt to revolutionize parcel delivery while cutting greenhouse gasses. According to the Wing website, "in the U.S. alone, 27% of the greenhouse gas emissions come from transportation." Their solution? Employ autonomous delivery drone services to "increase access to goods, reduce traffic congestion in cities, and help ease the CO_2 emissions attributable to the transportation of goods." According to X, these drones can fly up to 400 feet above the ground and can safely deliver a package to your front door step. In July 2018, Wing became an independent Alphabet (the parent corporation of Google) business.

Makani attempts to create renewable energy by using kites with small rotors tethered to an electricity-producing ground station. Will these projects deliver greater access to technology in rural areas in the world to come? Who knows. Still, the teams imagine audacious possibilities.

The ideas generated at X are the product of pure imagination. They attempt to apply imagination to solve some of the world's biggest problems in a commercially viable way. But none of those products have quite as much immediate commercial appeal as the self-driving car—at least, not as far as I'm concerned. Waymo, a self-driving-car company incubated for seven years at X, aims to produce the autonomous vehicles of the future. Its work has informed so much of the other thinking in the autonomous vehicle industry, including the thinking employed in those cars I see driving around the Strip District. And much of the work relating to self-driving cars happened under the eye of Dr. Teller.

Amid the global pandemic known as COVID-19,

high schools and universities around the world shuttered. Quarantines and lockdowns were imposed. Graduations were canceled. And in those strange days, many famous personalities and thinkers delivered virtual graduation addresses. One of those famed thinkers and personalities was Dr. Teller. In his commencement address, he outlined X initiatives that were the product of pure imagination, even though they never made it to the final stages of production.

There was the vertical farming initiative, which was envisioned to use ten times less water and 100 times less land than conventional farming. But staple crops—grains and rice—couldn't grow this way, and so the project was killed. Likewise, the team at X scrapped a promising lighter-than-air, variable-buoyancy cargo ship that would cut down the carbon footprint of shipping because the cost to produce the prototype was too expensive. How did these projects end up in the graveyard of good ideas? According to Teller, X cuts projects as soon as critical flaws are discovered. They change courses and modify approaches as soon as possible. What's more, they never penalize team members for recommending the termination of a project. In fact, X rewards it.

I spoke with Astro about the X team and their approach to solving the world's biggest problems. In his words, "The goal of X is to maximize both goodness in the world and value for Alphabet" (their parent company). So, he explained, if there are two moonshots on the table, both of which could make both a significant impact in the world and return a profit, they examine the reward-risk ratios. And even if one of those moonshots is riskier, if it has the potential to create more goodness in the world and more profit, they can pursue the moonshot, even if it sounds a little crazy.

Teller and his X team are reimagining the world. And with an almost acerbic tone, he tells me that most of corporate America has it wrong. The idea that profit and purpose are at odds is a "bad meme in the world," and X is setting out to disprove that meme. And that's when I asked his biggest idea, the moonshot that maximizes both profit and purpose. "I'm sorry to go meta on you," he said, "but it's what we've been talking about. I believe it's possible to build an organization that has a much more virtuous cycle with its employees, generates more value for its investors or parent company, and produces more goodness to the world—all at the same time." Then he put it straight: The moonshot he's willing to sacrifice all other moonshots for is inspiring other companies to do exactly what X is doing.

Teller and the team at X have set out to create a better world. And they do it by unleashing their imaginations, by imagining solutions that maximize goodness in the world while still returning a profit. They kill projects that won't work, but they don't let negativity limit their imaginations. Maybe most importantly, by pursuing their own moonshots, the people at X inspire us to chase ours.

A SOBER, FOCUSED, AND AUDACIOUS IMAGINATION LEADS TO BETTER REALITIES FOR HUMANKIND

In my twenties I bought into the fallacy Teller so quickly dismissed as a corporate meme—that profits and purpose were at odds. But now, out of cash, out of office desks, out of anything certain, we had no other option but to reimagine our business from the ground up, to start with a blank slate and ask what was possible. We had to take something broken and make something better.

We weren't the first to find ourselves in this position, and we won't be the last. And perhaps you're in that place right now. Your company may be out of money, or your neighborhood may be dilapidated. Your local education system, church, or synagogue might be hemorrhaging money or people. Your marriage might be falling apart. Or maybe you've simply lost the drive to produce results for a profit-first company, and it's driving you headlong into a quarter- or midlife crisis. Whatever the case may be, as you'll see throughout this book, when things get darkest, Refounders get to work. They take a hard look at the status quo and ask *what ought to be* instead of *what is.*

How? As I wrote in chapter 1, the Refounder's approach is rooted in four distinct actions.

1. REFOUNDERS AREN'T AFRAID TO TAKE A SOBER LOOK AT HARD REALITIES

Version 1.0 of our business was a bust. Our frenetic approach, affinity for drum circles, and hope in finding the pot of gold at the end of the rainbow had not paid off. Contrary to our belief, the dot-com revolution had not simplified the fundamentals of growing a business. In fact, the opposite was true, and there was no more hiding from it.

We stopped and took a sober look at the hard realities. We allowed the fear of failure to sink in. After all, Chris and I knew that if we didn't turn the ship around, we'd both be unemployed in the middle of a post-9/11 recession, a truly scary proposition. But instead of wallowing in that fear, we allowed it to motivate us to reimagine *what ought to be.* And though we didn't have our eyes set on a larger purpose yet, asking what ought to be would eventually lead us to the larger epiphany.

2. REFOUNDER'S FOCUS: RELEASE THE FALSE NARRATIVE OF BEING DIVERSIFIED

We were doing our best to be diversified, pursuing multiple products at a time. This was, perhaps, nothing more than a product of immature thinking. We'd been taught by so many— our parents, childhood teachers, even some college professors— to be well-rounded and not to put all our eggs in one basket. We took this message to heart, but not in the right ways.

When we're faced with a refounding opportunity, we have to sharpen our focus. We must exchange the many possibilities for the *right* possibility. As Greg McKeown, author of the book *Essentialism* says, we have to identify the "vital few from the trivial many." Of becoming an essentialist, McKeown writes,

> Essentialism is not about how to get more things done; it's about how to get the *right* things done. It doesn't mean just doing less for the sake of less, either. It is about making the wisest possible investment of your time and energy in order to operate at our highest point of contribution by doing only what is essential.[7]

---

7. Greg McKeown, *Essentialism: The Disciplined Pursuit of Less* (New York: Currency, 2014), 5.

True visionaries don't pursue the myth of diversification. They're not out to be all things to all customers. Like the teams at X, they focus on a small number of projects or ideas, and they try to maximize the potential of each. And if the potential can't be maximized, they kill the project. They pivot. The same was true for us. When we stopped trying to be all things to all potential customers and stakeholders, when we narrowed our focus, we were able to apply our imagination to what was vital. (We'll discuss this more in chapter 4.) That's when things started changing.

3. REFOUNDERS IMAGINE NEW POSSIBILITIES

In that moment of sobriety, with a sharpened focus, Chris and I sat across the table from one another and took stock of the raw materials. We'd recognized each other's strengths. He was steady, a skilled and innovative coder, and asked great questions. I brought positivity, abstract thinking, and creativity to the table. Together, we collaborated and thought through every side of a problem or opportunity. We knew the internet was still replete with promise and it would change the face of healthcare. What's more, we had a board of directors that believed in us enough to give us a shot at turning the company around. It wasn't much, but it was a start.

So, we set out to imagine a new future, one in which insights from our software led to better healthcare. We imagined new measurements of success and what it would take to get there. We envisioned a company that had made it through its dark night and had become a culture-impacting business. We asked what kind of company we'd want to be a part of. We took notes on what that kind of business might look like and set a course to get there. And we didn't limit our imaginations simply because we didn't know how we could achieve the outcomes.

Psychological research shows that each of us have a unique way of coping with both personal and professional adversity. Some cut and run. Some reimagine and fight for change. Some can't let go of the past. In a *Harvard Business Review* article, "How to Bounce Back from Adversity," Joshua Margolis and Paul Stoltz stated,

> [R]esilient managers move quickly from analysis to a plan of action (and reaction). After the onset of adversity, they shift from cause-oriented thinking to response-oriented thinking, and their focus is strictly forward.[8]

In other words, when trouble comes, resilient managers might ask "What happened?" but they do not dwell on the question. Instead, they turn to go-forward thinking. Resilient managers—Refounders, by my definition—imagine what could be and work toward achieving that possibility. While the past has its importance and place, Refounders work with intention toward a better future.

---

8. Joshua Margolis and Paul Stoltz, "How to Bounce Back from Adversity," *Harvard Business Review* (January-February 2010), https://hbr.org/2010/01/how-to-bounce-back-from-adversity (accessed November 15, 2020).

4. REFOUNDERS CREATE BETTER REALITIES FOR PEOPLE

Refounders don't just imagine increased earnings or product possibilities. They imagine a better world for the people in their businesses, neighborhoods, institutions of faith, and communities. And this imagination isn't limited to those who share their skin color, religious affiliation, social class, or political party. Refounders work toward the flourishing of all people, because when all people have the opportunity to thrive, their world flourishes.

In the first months of refounding, Chris and I couldn't have laid out these action steps for reimagining, not exactly. But looking back, I see this is exactly what we did. We took hold of hard realities, imagined better possibilities, narrowed our focus, and looked for ways to make the world better for the people in our industry, company, and community. We set our sights on the quadruple win—the win for the clients, the win for the employees, the win for the company leadership and investors, and the win for cities in which we operate. And now, I see how that imagination panned out.

Of course, we didn't know how much work it would take to bring that imagination to life. If we had, we might have taken our walking papers and hit the streets in search of the next opportunity. But then I would have missed the turnaround that reframed the way I view everything, the way I imagine making a difference in the world around me on a daily basis. However, reimagining a different reality was only the beginning. With just a hint of a new vision, it was time to get to work.

REFOUNDER TAKEAWAYS

- Refounders reject the notion that profit and purpose are at odds.
- Refounders do not focus on what is, but instead, focus on *what ought to be.*
- Refounders narrow their focus and advance products, purposes, and ideas that create better realities for people.

THREE

TACKLING PROBLEM ZERO

With layoffs behind us, we focused on what I've come to call Problem Zero. Problem Zero is the practical problem that threatens an organization's (or organism's) survival. Our Problem Zero? Our debt. If we couldn't get it under control, we were dead in the water, and we'd never achieve a successful refounding.

Within days of agreeing to the turnaround, we thumbed through a stack of unopened envelopes at the office. We looked at the dates, some of which went back more than four months. There were bills from vendors, from an attorney's office, from Einstein Bagels. There was a notice from the landlord. An unopened bill from the office furniture store that had already come to collect their belongings.

Aside from the payroll account, which received a $10,000 monthly injection from a board member to pay Chris and me, there was very little cash. And when I stacked cash reserves up against the mountain of debt, it was a gut punch. Not only were we cash-strapped, we were almost a half-million in debt.

I didn't know much about corporate financing options, and I knew even less about bankruptcy. Chuck, a forensic accountant on retainer and straight shooter, examined our spreadsheet and reviewed the underlying bills. He looked at our cash flow (or lack thereof) and examined the assets. He gave the company a financial checkup, and when he was finished, he confirmed what we already knew. We were insolvent and, short of a miracle, we were staring down the barrel of bankruptcy. If the company was going to make it another two months, we'd need our creditors—*all of them*—to restructure our debt. If three or more of them disagreed, we'd likely find ourselves plunged into an involuntary bankruptcy.

Pennies on the dollar. That's all we could pay. But if we could get our creditors to agree, we might have a shot.

I delivered the news to Anthony, the very man who had tasked us with leading the company refounding. He listened, digested the news, then said he knew exactly what to do. Before joining the board, he said, he'd spent a year and a half navigating a billion-dollar healthcare restructuring. It was one of the largest restructurings in the history of Pennsylvania, and he'd been the CEO through the process. He had real-life experience and had learned a thing or two about corporate debt restructuring.

"We'll get through this," he said, and I believed him.

First, he said, we needed to imagine the right outcome. To resolve Problem Zero, we needed each of the creditors to settle the debt for a fraction of the outstanding amount.

What's more, we'd need to do it quickly and with equal terms in case we had to declare bankruptcy. Under bankruptcy, he said, any preferential treatment of a creditor would be viewed with suspicion. "And Patrick," he said, "you're going to have to push hard to get this done."

Anthony described the best way to negotiate debt in step-by-step detail:

Step One: Make the introduction, tell the creditor I'd taken over as the president of the company.

Step Two: Apprise the creditor of our situation, filling in a few details, depending on the creditor.

Step Three: Mention the fact that we were trying to avoid bankruptcy. In fact, he said, use the word *bankruptcy* with convincing, repetitive authority.

Step Four: Tell them you're out of cash and need to settle the debt for less than eleven cents on the dollar.

Step Five: Hold your breath, bite your tongue, and wait for them to accept or reject your offer.

I took his marching orders, and in preparation to manage our debt, I plotted a scatter diagram that showed our list of creditors by the amount we owed. Einstein's Bagels was on the far left, and we owed them $128. On the far right was the law firm who'd done our corporate work since the inception of the company, and we owed them $277,000. The middle was populated by furniture companies, equipment leasing companies, and utility servicers. It was a tangle of debt, a Gordian knot, and we'd have to cut through it with surgical precision if we were to come out on the other side.

I was the suit-wearing president of a tech company, and still I knew the truth: I was nothing more than a twenty-something-year-old kid. The thought of going toe-to-toe with the manager of Einstein's Bagels felt awkward, which is to say nothing of negotiating against a high-powered attorney. Would any of those creditors negotiate with me?

Chris and I began working the phones. He called the copier company who did not take kindly to the news. Voices raised, they sparred. By the end of the call, the owner came to understand Chris was not bluffing, and that's when the situation softened. Eleven cents on the dollar would work, the owner said. But I shouldn't expect any favors in the future.

My phone conversation with the phone leasing company wasn't much better. They took days to evaluate our offer. In the end, they agreed, just as the copier company had.

The truth was, most of the vendors were much more understanding. In some cases, they were almost relieved that I'd reached out to them regarding the money they were owed, and virtually all of them were more sophisticated and experienced than I was in negotiating credits. In fact, most of the companies had reserves in place for bad debt, a concept that was foreign to me.

With the smaller debts out of the way, it was time to deal with the law firm. Complicating the enormity of the debt was the fact that one of the founding partners of the law firm sat on the board of our company. And though he had a professional relationship with Anthony, the two had decided that they would not communicate regarding debt negotiations. I would be the primary dealmaker along with another board member, Kirk. Another partner would be the primary dealmaker for the law firm. I was to go toe-to-toe with a seasoned, no-nonsense, bulldog-by-reputation transactional attorney. How?

The night before our scheduled meeting on one of the top floors of a large downtown building, I received a phone call from a brash, high-flying tech start-up founder, who was also on our board. Marcus was the kind of businessman who burned white-hot, and he wanted to give me practical negotiating advice.

"You know what you got to do, right?" he asked. "If you get to a standstill in the negotiations, if you can't break through, stand up, flip that f&@king table over, and walk out."

I nodded along on the other side of the phone, wondering if this was how to win friends and influence people, particularly in a debt negotiation. And the following day, I found myself sitting alone at a 30-foot mahogany table with delicately curved legs and an inlay so extravagant it might have been museum-worthy. As I waited for the attorney to enter, I grabbed the edge of the table and lifted. It didn't budge. So much for flipping tables. And it was at that precise moment that my adversary walked into the room.

I meant to walk him through my step-by-step process, but he took the bull by the horns, told me they were entitled to 100 cents on the dollar. I stammered, told him we simply didn't have the cash, but before I got to the point of my script where I discussed bankruptcy, he said, "I'm sure you're about to tell me you're insolvent, but why should I care?" There was no good answer for this, of course, and so, instead of trying to rebut him, I set out to see whether there was any negotiating room.

For hours we struggled, searching for a compromise. I walked him through the numbers, showed him the bleakness of the situation. Terms started coming together. I began feeling my oats. I was going blow for blow with one of the city's toughest attorneys, and we were crafting a great deal. Then, my ego got the best of me. I looked over his shoulder, saw downtown Pittsburgh sprawling out the window below us. He had it all—money, position, power, prestige. I had little more than a mountain of debt and my pride, and for pride's sake, I wanted to win. And so, I changed my negotiation strategy.

I wanted a better deal, I said, changing the terms to something I'd proposed almost an hour earlier. It must have been the straw that broke the camel's back, because he stood, leaned across that mahogany inlay, and said, "Patrick, if you change your position one more time, I'm going to walk across the room and punch you in the nose." His tone was flat, his face even flatter. His right fist became a tight ball, and he pressed his knuckles into the table. It was the look of a practiced brawler, and as I stood in that icy stare, I knew the negotiations were just about finished.

The agreement with the law firm wasn't like the other deals I'd negotiated. We would pay a negotiated lump sum to the law firm each year for the next three years. The firm would write off a chunk of the debt, too, and what they'd written off would be given back to them via an equity stake in the company. It was a fair deal for them, and it gave us the ability to fight another day, even if it created a cash crunch. And as I stood in the elevator and made my way to the ground floor, something like relief washed over me.

We were on our way to overcoming our foundational problem, our Problem Zero. Maybe we really were making this thing work.

THE OPIOID EPIDEMIC: DEFINING PROBLEM ZERO

Refounders often take on the impossible. Turning around a failing company, a failing community, or even a failing marriage requires negotiating immense complexity. And making great strides toward accomplishing impossible tasks requires a clearly defined Problem Zero (the practical problem that threatens survival).

In our case, Problem Zero was easy to define: Our debt was choking us. Anthony helped us imagine the correct outcome and formulate an approach to solving the task. Chris and I were dedicated to negotiating the debt. Though our particular problem was debt negotiation, Refounders apply this approach to all manner of problems. And the more impossible the problem, the more dedicated true Refounders are to resolving it.

Consider Justin Moore. The chief executive officer of the American Physical Therapy Association and an outside-the-box thinker, he is dedicated to advancing integrated, holistic human health. What is one of the primary threats to human health in modern America? The opioid epidemic.

Over the years, I've spoken with Justin, and he's shared some startling insights. The majority of Americans will struggle with pain, most notably low back pain, at some point during their life. Of that majority, most will first see their primary care physicians for pain management. And in modern healthcare, primary care physicians often turn first to pharmacological solutions, namely, writing a prescription for opioids.

But there is a better way. Physical therapy can be used before either pharmacological or surgical interventions to treat pain, with better long-term outcomes for the patient. In fact, a study conducted by the Moran Company indicated that the use of physical therapy as a first intervention for lower back pain resulted in 19% lower costs to the Medicare program when compared with injections as a first intervention, and 75% lower costs when compared with surgery as a first intervention.[9] So why doesn't the healthcare industry mandate (or at least include) physical therapy before pills are prescribed, particularly when the outcomes prove its efficacy?

To answer that question, I called Justin.

After exchanging pleasantries, I put the question to him. Why doesn't the medical community require physical therapy before opioid prescription? He doesn't balk, says physical therapy has historically been used for post-injury rehabilitation. And truth be told, he says, most patients who attend post-surgical physical therapy have already been prescribed opioids, whether for post-surgical pain management or long-term pain management. And though not all physical therapy patients will become addicted to those drugs, a large number will.

It's a segmented approach to pain management, he says. A prescribe-first, cut-first approach. And this approach has exacerbated opioid addiction in America. But if the medical community could be more integrated, if physical therapists could be brought in much earlier in the process, he believes opioid addiction could be reduced dramatically.

In an effort to support his hypothesis with numbers, he

---

9. Moran Company, "Initial Treatment Intervention and Average Total Medicare A/B Costs for FFS Beneficiaries with an Incident Low Back Pain (Lumbago) Diagnosis in CY 2014," Prepared for Alliance for Physical Therapy Quality and Innovation (APTQI), May 2017, https://www.aptqi.com/Resources/documents/APTQI-Complete-Study-Initial-Treatment-Intervention-Lumbago-May-2017.pdf (accessed November 15, 2020).

sends a series of medical studies. Though the United States has less than 5% of the world's population, it consumes over 80% of the world's opioid supply. Over 12 million Americans reported long-term opioid use or misuse in 2015, the studies show. What's more, The National Survey on Drug Use and Health reported over 42,000 prescription opioid-related deaths in 2016, with total estimated costs of prescription opioid use reaching . . . $78.5 billion.[10] Talk about a drain on the economy. And what's among the most common reasons for prescription opioids? Low back pain.

Prescription opioids are among the most frequently prescribed medications for treatment of low back pain, and more than half of opioid users report having a history of back pain. This is particularly concerning because "[Low back pain] is one of the three most common conditions for which Americans seek medical care."

Justin shares that the American College of Physicians and the Centers for Disease Control both recommend non-pharmacological treatments for low back pain. What do they recommend? Physical therapy, exercise, and massage. In fact, these organizations recommend that opioids should not be used until these sorts of less-invasive treatments fail. Why? Because these same studies show that patients who first visit a physical therapist for low back pain experience relief from their pain, are less likely to experience short-term and long-term opioid use, and ultimately spend less money on long-term care. Put another way, their health outcomes are much better.

---

10. Substances Abuse and Mental Health Services Administration (SAMHSA), "Results from the 2016 National Survey on Drug Use and Health: Detailed Tables," (September 7, 2017), https://www.samhsa.gov/data/sites/default/files/NSDUH-DetTabs-2016/NSDUH-DetTabs-2016.pdf (accessed November 15, 2020).

The takeaway? We have an opioid problem here in America, one that's an enormous drain on our economy. And why is it so prevalent? Moore indicates that it's because the American healthcare system has taken the wrong approach to treating pain. Physical therapy for low back pain is historically an afterthought, he says, even though involving physical therapists at the earliest stages increases mobility, stimulates healing, and often alleviates the need for surgical interventions or chemical pain management.

As I listen, I note America's Problem Zero as it relates to early alternatives to the opioid epidemic: the over-prescription of opioids in modern America. And if the science shows that physical therapy could be integrated earlier into pain management to reduce the need for opioid prescriptions, how can Moore and others get physical therapists involved earlier in pain management cases? This is the question Moore is asking.

As the CEO for the APTA, Moore is pushing for change. The organization is lobbying for policy reforms, pushing insurance providers, lawmakers, and regulators to use alternative interventions as a frontline treatment for chronic and low back pain. Second, the APTA is investing heavily in health research in an effort to show that every dollar paid for physical therapy before pharmacological and surgical intervention saves multiple dollars to the healthcare system and the patient, including addiction-related treatments. Finally, the organization encourages healthier lifestyles via a public relations campaign promoting exercise, better diets, and physical therapy.

Moore is taking a Refounder's approach to tackling the opioid epidemic. He sees how the healthcare industry's nonintegrated approach to chronic pain exacerbates the opioid epidemic. He knows physical therapy can play a role in reducing that epidemic. And so, with a clearly defined Problem Zero, an imagined better outcome, and a plan of attack for achieving that outcome, he's gotten to work. He's attempting to restore the virtuous cycle to healthcare, the cycle that treats the patient as a whole person. He's taking something that's broken—the healthcare system as it relates to opioid addiction—and recreating something better. And though the change is incremental, he's already seeing results.

ATTACKING PROBLEM ZERO: THE REFOUNDER'S APPROACH

Failure is a fact of life. It is painful. But it's not uncommon. Failure visits businesses, neighborhoods, political parties, and entire systems, like healthcare. And though there can be many reasons underlying any failure, they all have one thing in common: there are flaws in the system.

Failing businesses hemorrhage money.

Failed neighborhoods lose people.

Failed political parties don't turn out the vote.

A failing healthcare system creates undesirable outcomes, like opioid addiction.

When a system is failing, Refounders get to work. How?

1. TAKE A SOBER LOOK: REFOUNDERS DEFINE PROBLEM ZERO

Refounders do not shoot first and ask questions later. They do not ignore Problem Zero. They do not manipulate numbers or spin facts in an attempt to avoid dealing with it, either. Instead, Refounders stop and take a sober look and try to understand and clearly define their Problem Zero. They state it clearly, too. After all, as Charles Kettering, an inventor with more than 186 patents, said, "A problem well-stated is half-solved."

As we looked to refound, we took a sober look at the primary obstacle to survival: our expenses. There were other problems to be sure—we were short on product offerings and had no real source of income—but we began by clearly defining and stating our Problem Zero, the fundamental problem that, if overcome, allows for growth.

I might define the American Physical Therapy Association's contribution to solving the opioid epidemic (a modern healthcare Problem Zero) as, "How to introduce physical therapy earlier in pain-management cycles to reduce resulting opioid addiction and surgical procedures." With a clearly defined Problem Zero and a means of contributing to the solution, they can work to achieve better outcomes.

2. REFOUNDER'S FOCUS: SOLVING PROBLEM ZERO BY WORKING BACKWARD

In the course of my career, I've met more than a few Refounders whose Problem Zero was just like ours. They needed to shave expenses, reduce outflows. And sometimes, it's simply a numbers game, simply trimming the fat. But more often than not, drastic actions need to be taken. Sometimes, you have to reimagine the world and work backward.

How?

Skilled Refounders examine Problem Zero with a simple question in mind: *What ought to be?* For Net Health, the question was simple: *What ought our balance sheet debt be if we were going to survive?* The American Physical Therapy Association might ask a different question: *What ought the place of physical therapy be in the care continuum, particularly for pain management?* And once a Refounder clearly answers what ought to be, they can create a step-by-step course to achieve the *ought* despite the *is*.

This approach—asking *What ought to be?* and charting a course in reverse—must apply to the entire Problem Zero, but it also applies to the myriad minute problems within Problem Zero. In our case, for instance, we had a very large expense to a very hard-nosed creditor. What was true? We owed a lot of money, and it appeared that the only way out was bankruptcy. But what ought to have been true? There ought to have been a win-win, a creative way to give everyone a chance to succeed. And thinking through what ought to be, we negotiated a creative restructuring that gave us some relief with the law firm. The shift in mindset paved the way for resolution.

3. IMAGINING NEW POSSIBILITIES: REBELS DON'T IMAGINE ALONE

Over the years, I've watched too many organizations hemorrhage cash and assume the only solution is to secure more money. Focused on *what is,* they negotiate outcomes from the present instead of an imagined future.

Refounders are what I call "the rebels of ought." They don't accept the mediocrity of what is, but instead, turn their imaginations for creative solutions toward what ought to be. And when their imagination runs dry, they learn from others and allow the expertise of coworkers, consultants, and mentors to inform their imaginations. This is true for every problem solver, even the geniuses in the room.

In September 2020, a team of computer scientists at Carnegie Mellon University solved "Keller's conjecture," a geometry problem that has stumped some of the greatest mathematical minds. It's a problem so complex that John Mackey, a teaching professor in CMU's Computer Science Department and Department of Mathematical studies, has been trying to solve the problem for over thirty years. Mackey couldn't solve the problem alone. He invited Marijn Heule, a CMU associate professor of computer science who imagined the approach to understanding Keller's conjecture. Heule used a particular program (an SAT solver, for those of you into computer science and mathematics) to complete the problem. Interviewed about the problem, Heule indicated:

> There are many ways to make these transla-
> tions, and the quality of the translation typi-
> cally makes or breaks your ability to solve the
> problem. . . . The reason we succeeded is that
> John has decades of experience and insight
> into this problem, and we were able to trans-
> form it into a computer-generated search.[11]

Mackey needed Heule's programming expertise to imagine a better problem-solving approach. Heule needed Mackey's experience and insight into the problem to solve the problem. Neither had the tools to solve the problem alone. Only together were they successful.

---

11. Paul Guggenheimer, "Carnegie Mellon University Scientists Solve 90-Year-Old Math Puzzle," Triblive (September 30, 2020), https://triblive.com/local/cmu-scien-tists-solve-90-year-old-math-puzzle/.

There are times we can solve Problem Zero without input. But more often than not, once our Problem Zero is defined, solutions are better imagined in teams. That's what happened at Net Health. Anthony helped me imagine possible solutions using his deep well of knowledge. And though Chris and I owned the actual negotiation process, I cannot take credit for the imagined outcome. The imagined outcome was a team effort, and that team was led by an experienced Rebel of Ought.

4. CREATING BETTER REALITIES: PUT YOUR IMAGINATION TO ACTION

Refounders chart more creative courses toward better solutions. And if they have to rebel against conventional wisdom, if they have to be a grain of sand in the machine, they aren't afraid to do it. They act on their imagination, particularly when that imagination has been curated in a team environment. Refounders engage in difficult negotiations, attack seemingly impossible problems, and act to bring their imaginations to life. And when those in the world around them see the outcomes they achieve, they'll often say, "I never saw that coming."

The process of reducing expenses through creative negotiation taught me there's always a way to get to the ought, even if I had to endure the threat of getting punched to do it. It taught me more, too.

Through the process of negotiating our Problem Zero, we experienced the outcome we needed. What's more, though, I grew personally.

What do I mean?

I learned humility. Admitting failure wasn't easy, especially as a young professional trying to make a name in the world. But traveling from company to company asking for mercy started to undo some of my pride. And as I grew in humility, I noticed some of my more unsavory characteristics starting to wane— arrogance, greed, thirst for importance.

I also learned about grace, how, for the most part, business owners were willing to work with me, and that was something I hadn't expected to find. In college, I'd imagined the business world as merciless, as full of characters like Gordon Gekko from the movie *Wall Street*. The reality was far different. The best businesses were human-centered and offered grace to those struggling. And when it came down to it, even that law firm exercised a measure of grace, though they could have taken us for every penny we were worth. And today, my experiences with those companies remind me that when a legitimate Refounder comes knocking, asking for a little grace in the way I deal with him and his outstanding debts, I should extend it whenever possible.

I learned that for the Refounder there will always be a new Problem Zero. When faced with it, the Refounder will constantly ask *What ought to be?* and work backward to chart a better course. The Refounder, in essence, is always attuned to this way of thinking.

I learned, too, that laughter really is good medicine. Sitting there tearing open dozens of envelopes, each one revealing a bleaker and bleaker situation, we found ourselves occasionally unable to stop laughing. We realized that what we were doing appeared completely insane. And when I was able to share a chuckle with a creditor, when we exchanged smiles or told a light-hearted anecdote in the midst of difficult negotiations, I realized that a smile, a laugh, can go a long way toward making an insufferable situation bearable. And learning to laugh in a hard situation can sometimes bring a great deal of healing, even if you don't realize it in the moment.

In essence, I learned what ought to be within our company itself. I also learned what ought to be part of my character.

In the months before writing this book, I was invited to give the opening remarks for a speech by Ray Betler, a friend whom I admire. Ray is the now-retired CEO of Wabtec, a $14+ billion company with 18,000 employees. The lecture was held at the Duquesne Club, an historic place where Pittsburgh's businesspeople and entrepreneurs have gathered to share ideas and network for over 150 years. There I was, surrounded by the mahogany columns, tapestried walls, and rare art. Suited up preparing to deliver my remarks, rehearsing a few prepared comments, I looked across the room and saw a familiar face. The lawyer who'd once threatened to punch me in the nose was sitting in a dining room chair, speaking to a colleague, and both were awaiting my speech. I smiled, remembering our negotiation many years ago, and then turned to the podium.

After the speech, he found me, asked how I was doing. I told him things were going well for the company, keeping it short because I sensed ne was in a hurry. He nodded his approval, leaned in like he did all those years ago across the conference table. This time, he didn't threaten me, though. Instead, he said, "It's unbelievable what you've done."

It wasn't much, but that day, it meant the world. He'd had a front-row seat to the story of our corporate refounding. As he turned to leave the club, I realized that none of our success would have been possible if the three of us hadn't sat down at the table and negotiated Problem Zero from the foundational premise of *What ought to be*. He had partnered with me in the Refounding. Thinking of that, I smiled.

REFOUNDER TAKEAWAYS

- Refounders identify Problem Zero, the problem that threatens an organization's survival.
- Refounders imagine a solution to Problem Zero, then ask what must be true to achieve that solution.
- Refounders do not act alone. Instead, they take a team approach to solving their biggest problems.

FOUR

REFOUNDERS REFINE

One year into our turnaround, our business was reminiscent of Pittsburgh in the early 1980s, just before its tech rebirth. We were still in the corporate version of a recession, but we'd identified Problem Zero and solved it. We'd negotiated a controlled default on our previous office space, a space in a swanky downtown joint we had no business leasing. (It was the first and last time I had an office with an *en suite* bathroom, except for when I occasionally worked from my bedroom during COVID.) Now, we were set up in an old warehouse building in the Strip District.

These were the days before the Strip was revitalized, and the neighborhood was rough. A dead body had been found in the building next door only months before, and many of the buildings were ramshackle, to say the least. Our new office—a warehouse built in 1920—had just been renovated but still had old bones. And even though it wasn't as posh as our previous office building, there was an upshot. The space was quiet. And so, with less noise, less debt, and a few more months of leeway, Chris and I turned to our core business.

Months before the move, we'd leapt to phase two of the plan: refine our product offerings, identify the one with the best potential, and get it to market. We weren't short of ideas. In fact, we had too many. Three were viable, though.

Product #1: an alternative medicine portal inspired by Dr. Lewis Mehl-Madrona's natural healing work. The good doctor—a Native American—had studied the healing practices of the Lakota, Cherokee, and Cree traditions. There was a growing market of people exploring alternatives to modern America's Big Medicine complex, and an online portal connecting patients to healers across the country might be a boon. Still, we couldn't conceptualize a clear product. Was there opportunity in developing the hub? Was it in creating some sort of tracking software for alternative medicine providers? And even if we could identify the product, how would we charge for it? It was too murky, so we moved on.

Sorry, Dr. Mehl-Madrona.

Product #2: a software system that tracked the Minimum Data Set (MDS) required by Medicaid or Medicare for all eligible residents of long-term care facilities (then known as nursing homes). The system was designed to assist the country's 16,000 skilled nursing facilities track the physical, psychological, and psycho-social functioning of the patients and prepared the patient data for direct transmission to the government, cutting down on the time it took to receive Medicare or Medicaid reimbursements. As an added benefit, the process would keep the nursing care facilities in compliance with federally mandated regulations. *SmartCare*, as the product was known, wasn't sexy, but maybe it was viable? Still, it would take massive market saturation in the very competitive field of nursing care services. Could we reach the kind of scale and saturation we needed to survive?

Product #3: Again targeted to nursing care and other long-term care facilities, this old-school, paper-based system provided a color-coded assessment for patient at-risk for in-house-acquired pressure ulcers—the technical term for a bedsore. This provided a simple key for the nurses to identify patients who needed to be checked, turned, or treated. Responding to the codes, the nurses could decrease the number of bedsores in their patient population and increase the comfort of their residents. If they responded to the codes correctly, it would cut down on the number of bedsore lawsuits brought by family members, a particular source of litigation in the late 1990s and early 2000s. Still, we were met with the same challenge. How would we achieve any sort of market saturation?

With two viable potential products, we were still at loggerheads. There were good ideas, even executable ones. But could we get them to market?

And as we discussed the very real limitations—we needed cashflow *now* without needing to achieve significant market saturation—it was clear what we needed. We needed a niche where we could survive and thrive, one where we could carve out a competitive advantage in an underserved field. And as luck or fate would have it, that solution presented itself.

We'd become aware of a small but growing field of medicine—chronic wound care treatment. Within that space, we'd taken note of a company that had established a cutting-edge method for treating chronic wounds in which the doctors created a sort of gooey ointment by spinning down the patient's white blood cells in a centrifuge. When applied to the wound, that goo was said to increase healing rates, and because it was made from the patient's own white blood cells, the risk of an adverse reaction was lower.

We saw the establishment of a market, one we knew we could serve. And though we didn't have a point of introduction with the company, though it would fold due to alleged mismanagement only months later, it opened our eyes to a new possibility. And so, when I was introduced to one of their primary competitors in Southern California, I was ready.

Over the phone, I listened to the nurse explain their model. They were also on the cutting edge of wound care treatment. Their approach was novel. Their research was solid. But as I spoke to the nurse, as I peppered her with questions, I discovered they needed help. They needed software to track patient progress. Knowing they operated twenty-seven clinics, I ran the quick math. If I could get a simple version of our wound care software installed at every facility, we might be able to turn the corner and get our company in the black. And so, I asked for an introduction to the clinic's founder.

Weeks later, Chris and I flew to the office in southern California, and I sat across from the founder. Leaned back in his office chair, shirt open and gold medallion resting on his well-tanned skin, he asked me about my background, my family, my work history. I answered as best I could, glancing at the two photos on the credenza behind him—one of his jet and one of his yacht.

Preliminary questions out of the way, he shared more of his backstory. He was the inventor of the modern hyperbaric chamber, he said, and he'd built his company on that technology. He was convinced his new wound care therapy could significantly improve the quality of life of those suffering from chronic wounds. He needed a software solution.

I made the pitch, told him we'd developed software that could track the size, history, and healing curve of any given wound. What's more, it was connected to the internet, which meant it could generate reports to compare physician efficacy and benchmark wound-healing rates. We could give his people the tools they needed to measure healing and run their operations. It was a clear win.

He listened, asked questions, and showed an agility and understanding of the issues and the technology. I had him on the hook. I could feel it. But when I finished the presentation, I realized the truth—he had me on the hook too.

"Here's the pitch," he said. "Let us use your software in a few of our facilities for ninety days, no charge. We'll tell you what we think, and we can negotiate after that."

We were on the cusp of our first large sale, but what was his angle? Was he hoping to use the product for ninety days for free, then convince us we should pay him to improve it? Worse yet, was he hoping to crib the software suite altogether? After all, this wouldn't be hard for a business person of his caliber. He had the cash to pull a coup, and we didn't have the war chest to stop him. I didn't have time for his game, whatever the game was, so I countered hard.

"I can't do that. Here's what I can do, though. We can install our software in every location within ninety days. We can't do it for free, but we'll discount our fee. "

He needed us. We needed him. We both knew it. He extended his hand and we shook on it. We had a deal. This contract would give us enough working capital to hire our third employee and still leave cash flow to increase our reserves. He said his lawyers would draw up the paperwork. I thanked him. And with that, we were off to the races.

REFOUNDERS REFINE IDEAS TO WIN

Refounders tackle Problem Zero, the fundamental problem that short-circuits any refounding attempt, which gives them the opportunity to take on a larger refounding. But tackling your Problem Zero doesn't mean it goes away forever. In fact, if you are successful in making progress, new Problem Zeros will crop up as you solve complex, multivariate problems.

What's more, in complex structures and systems, a single Problem Zero might be all but impossible to define. There might be a myriad of problems, all acting in concert, all threatening the structure or system. In those situations, multiple solutions to these myriad problems might present themselves. And in those moments, you might be tempted to chase them all, but in the end, following the wrong ideas costs time, effort, and money. Refounders in complex systems know this, and instead of trying to tackle every problem simultaneously, they pick one problem, analyze it, and get to work, even if they might not define it as the Problem Zero underlying all of their problems. In other words, in these kinds of situations, rarely is there a meta–Problem Zero. No one knows this better than John Wallace, a native of Pittsburgh's Homewood neighborhood.

Located on the east end of the city, Homewood was once a wealthy district. Andrew Carnegie, George Westinghouse, and Henry J. Heinz lived there in the late 1800s, as did many of their well-heeled contemporaries. In the early 1900s, Homewood continued growing, mostly as a result of German, Irish, and Italian immigrants along with middle-class Black families. But in the 1950s the city pushed many Black families from Pittsburgh's lower Hill District to make way for the Civic Arena, and Homewood became their landing place. And because the Pittsburghers of the day maintained their own stubborn prejudices, many of the white families who populated Homewood fled to suburban communities. It was an early form of "white flight," and by the 1960 census, Homewood's population had declined by more than 10 percent, and over 66 percent of the district's residents were African American.

The assassination of Dr. Martin Luther King Jr. in 1968 brought two days of demonstrations. Riots and looting broke out. Businesses were destroyed. Then, after the Fair Housing Act was passed, along with the Civil Rights Act in 1968, wealthier Black families in Homewood were allowed to integrate into wealthier (and predominantly white) communities. Some moved to the inner-ring suburbs like Penn Hills, even as white families moved further out. As a result, Homewood's economic health was decimated. By the 2000 census, the neighborhood was home to only 9,300 residents, over 98 percent of whom were African American. By 2010, the population declined to approximately 6,600. Many were impoverished.

John Wallace has an insider's perspective on Homewood. His grandfather—born in Alabama to the son of a freed slave—worked in the U.S. Steel coke ovens in Clairton, some fifteen miles south of Pittsburgh. Those beehive ovens with open flames produced something close to hellfire, Wallace said. The manager of the furnace once told Wallace's grandfather he was good enough to be a foreman, if only he weren't Black. Ceilings on opportunities for African Americans in those days were much lower, and those ceilings were harsh realities for those across the country.

John's grandfather only had an eighth-grade education, and John's father dropped out of high school to support his widowed mother and younger siblings. So, when John—who'd been raised in Homewood—was the first in his family to graduate from college, when he received his doctorate from the University of Michigan, when he accepted a job at the same university, he became a family success story. But years into his academic career, he felt the pull of his community. And when a job opened up at the University of Pittsburgh, he packed a Penske and moved his family from Ann Arbor back to the Steel City.

Wallace could have been content to move back to Pittsburgh and live a quiet suburban life. He could have turned his back on Homewood, but he didn't. Instead, he was determined to help refound his beloved yet struggling childhood neighborhood.

I heard Wallace, a sociologist by training, speak for the first time at a conference a few years back. Within minutes of his taking the mic, I knew I needed to pay attention. He shared his background, how he'd made his way through Michigan and back to his hometown. He was quick-witted, razor sharp, and he shared the truth in an approachable way.

With conviction, Wallace shared the realities of Homewood. It was an asset-rich, predominantly African American community with a proud history and good people. Like many of Pittsburgh's neighborhoods, though, it had suffered the brunt of the closing of the steel mills and the loss of over 150,000 jobs between the late 1970s and the mid 1980s. And hit by high levels of job loss, the crack epidemic, racial residential segregation, and lack of access to capital and other social problems, the neighborhood fell on hard times. Educational opportunities were limited, as were other civic services.

What's more, home ownership in Homewood was a significant issue. While the average home sale price for a home in Homewood was a mere fraction of the average price of a home in the greater City of Pittsburgh, many Homewood residents couldn't get financing to purchase the homes. Why? Because banks wouldn't make small loans on housing units, loans often as low as $35,000. As a result, only those with cash or hard-money lenders could afford to own property in Homewood, and those buyers often lived out of state and bought the properties for investment purposes. And once those homes were bought, the owners turned and leased them back to residents for over $1,000 per unit, though a portion of that rent was subsidized by the federal department of Housing and Urban Development. So, though the average Homewood lender could have owned the home for as little as $350 a month if they could have only received financing, they were now leasing property while their payments were siphoned off to out-of-state investors.

Many of the properties in the neighborhood weren't well-maintained by those investors. In fact, according to an article in the *Pittsburgh Post-Gazette*, one of those multi-tenant, out-of-state owned properties earned an inspection score of 9 on a 100-point scale. Those investors were, in fact, slumlords, and as a result, the residents of those properties were forced to relocate.

It was a vicious cycle, caused in large part by systemic racism that enslaved Black people for nearly 250 years and denied them access to education, paid employment, entre-preneurship, legal marriage, or access to capital. And because the properties were owned by others as passive income generators, the owners weren't incentivized to care for the properties. So, the neighborhood continued to decline. But housing wasn't the only issue. Wallace described a litany of problems faced by the Homewood residents—low employ-ment, substandard education, crime. There were several solutions for each, but simply throwing money at the prob-lems wouldn't create sustainable change. So, he and a group of Homewood residents, largely members of his church, began tackling the problems together, one by one. He laid out the work they'd done—neighborhood beautification, food cultivation, a school busing program. He showed the impact, too. Children were receiving education, and a dent was being made in food insecurity.

Wallace wrapped up his speech, and as he walked from the stage, the crowd applauded. As I joined them, something stirred. I needed to meet Wallace for myself and ask whether I could pick his brain about the refounding of Homewood.

Months later, I was invited to participate in a conference in Atlanta focused on using for-profit work to advance the social good. The invitation was extended to 300 speakers and business leaders from around the country who were using their platforms to share the good news of socially focused entrepreneurship. As chance would have it, John Wallace was seated at the table with me. We sat through the conference, and during the breaks, I asked him question after question. He shared the impact of the programs he'd started in Homewood, how each began with the simplest, most refined solution to some clearly defined problem. And each solution had a unified purpose—namely, to redeem the neighborhood, even if just a little. He shared his underlying philosophy, too, which was to redeem broken systems, and ultimately, make earth like heaven—beautiful, equitable, and just. And when he'd come back to Homewood, that's exactly what he and his congregation had set out to do.

Wallace returned home as an academic, but he'd also accepted the position as senior pastor of the church where he was raised—Bible Center Church in the heart of Homewood—and he began setting this heaven-on-earth vision. Because of practical constraints—budget and manpower—they'd begin in the simplest way. They'd work toward improving the physical appearance of Homewood.

The people of Bible Center Church asked *What ought to be?* and though they had numerous problems to address, they started at the simplest place—neighborhood cleanup. Their neighborhood ought to be a beautiful place to live. It ought to be a place the residents could take pride in. And though they could have lobbied the city for better policing or street cleaning or whatever, they started with a more refined idea. Donning T-shirts with the "Bible Center Church Loves Homewood" on the front and *"The church has left the building"*

on the back, Wallace and his crew began a Homewood beautification initiative. They cleaned their church grounds and
building, redeeming the physical appearance of one of the
anchoring structures in the neighborhood. From there, they
moved into the community, picking up trash, mowing vacant
lots, purchasing vacant and abandoned buildings. And when
some building they didn't own needed cleaning? They did it
anyway, trespassing when necessary, because, as Wallace said,
"the world is God's and everything in it, and as a practical
matter, what police officer in their right mind would bother us
for cleaning up the block?"

This is not to say the people of Bible Center Church
weren't addressing other issues, too. They were. But even as
they considered solutions or these other problems and worked
toward those solutions, they kept their focus on their refined
approach to beautification. They continued to clean up the
neighborhood one block at a time.

With the Homewood restoration underway, and with sights
set on laying the foundation for even more transformational
work, the church purchased a dilapidated triplex across the street,
a place where drug deals and prostitution were common. They
renovated the triplex, which became a space for community
programs. They hosted a community cookout, inviting the
neighbors for hotdogs and hamburgers so they could share
about the community services they intended to offer. From the
simplest idea—redeeming the beauty of Homewood—they'd
expanded their efforts to creating a sense of community. And as
they did, a new mindset began to take hold.

Wallace and his church would go on to start other community projects—a busing project aimed at getting kids to

school, after-school and summer programs to keep kids off the streets, a solar-powered aquaponic farm that produces fresh vegetables and attracts neighborhood residents who marvel at the self-contained ecosystem. But they didn't start with these more involved projects. Instead, they started with the simplest, most refined idea—make Homewood a beautiful place to live.

John Wallace, Bible Center Church and other congregations in and around Homewood, Homewood residents, local government officials, and not-for-profits, foundations, businesses and universities have come together to take something broken and create something better, something more beautiful. Over the years, as our relationship has grown, John has shown me the power of attacking any problem (including any Problem Zero) with a refined idea. He's shown me that when faced with a problem, you have to analyze it, pick a problem, and begin to execute. And what's true of John Wallace's approach to community development holds true for product ideas and business solutions. I know, because I've experienced it.

1. TAKE A SOBER LOOK: REDUCE THE NOISE

There are times when there's a clear Problem Zero, a problem you have to tackle in order to survive. At Net Health, we had a defined Problem Zero and we reduced the noise around us in order to solve it. We carved out time, took a break from the hustle, and examined our products from top to bottom, ranking them from least to most viable. Without reducing the noise, we might have kept chasing too many products and missed the primary opportunity when it presented itself.

In a sense, Wallace reduced the noise, too. Because they lived in a complex neighborhood, one facing many issues, there wasn't an easily definable Problem Zero. They could have begun providing any number of services to the community—and in fact, they'd go on to do just that—but they started simply. They began by focusing on the need for neighborhood beautification.

By reducing the noise and focusing on one problem, Refounders are able to come up with potential solutions. What are some practical ways to reduce the noise?

Research has shown clear links between taking strategic breaks throughout the day and employee engagement and productivity. And if I've learned anything, it's that making space, ideally offsite in a creative setting, helps set the stage for new thinking. Bill Gates is famous for taking "Think Weeks," where he retreats to a remote cabin in the woods to consider potential innovations.[12] But even if you can't retreat to woods for an entire week, you can take a simpler approach to reducing the noise so that you think through your most pressing problems. Book a hotel for a night, turn off all your electronics to minimize distractions, and think through a critical refinement question.

What if you can't give up a full night? Consider following my lead and take a multi-hour trip to a local coffee shop. Sitting in a secluded corner, I turn off my phone, turn off notifications on my computer, and let the ambient noise wash over

---

12. Catherine Clifford, "Bill Gates Took Solo 'Think Weeks' in a Cabin in the Woods—Why's It's a Great Strategy," CNBC.com (July 28, 2019) https://www.cnbc.com/2019/07/26/bill-gates-took-solo-think-weeks-in-a-cabin-in-the-woods.html.

me as I refine ideas down to their simplest form.[13]

What if your project is a group effort? Gather the team for an uninterrupted block of time. Turn off your smartphones, computers, anything that distracts you. Sit around the table. Focus on the problem at hand and brainstorm solutions. See what solutions present themselves when you reduce the noise.

2. REFOUNDER'S FOCUS: KILL YOUR DARLINGS

There's a simple saying in writing circles: "Kill your darlings." It's a phrase attributed to William Faulkner, Oscar Wilde, and more recently, to Stephen King who wrote, "kill your darlings, kill your darlings, even when it breaks your egocentric little scribbler's heart, kill your darlings."[14] The meaning? Sometimes, writers must strike passages they love, particularly if those passages detract from the work as a whole.

The same is true of products, programs, and ideas. Often met with many good options, a Refounder might need to hone his or her focus. They might need to kill a darling or two in order to pivot toward the smaller, but ultimately *better* idea.

Though Net Health had a working software prototype that would track patient issues, we realized the long-term care market was too saturated. Sure, if we could have broken in and established a footprint in that industry, we might have excelled, but we had neither the time nor the staff to make the play. We needed to identify a smaller niche, something with

---

13. As I write this, we're in the middle of the COVID-19 pandemic, and so I've curtailed this practice. I suppose this pandemic might continue indefinitely, but in the interim, you can still practice reducing the noise. Travel to a public park, turn off your phone, and refine, refine, refine.

14. Stephen King, *On Writing: A Memoir of the Craft* (New York: Scribner's, 2000), 222.

more bang for the buck, and we'd need to develop a simple product to fit that niche. So, we killed our other product offerings and focused on finding that niche. Ultimately, our pivot was a gamble, but it paid off.

Even if you don't kill your darlings, those darlings might need to be shoved into a closet, at least for a time. Wallace and his group didn't give up on the bigger problems facing Homewood, problems like education, crime, and food security. But they started at the simplest place and expanded from there. And if I had my guess, they aren't finished dreaming up new solutions to the most daunting problems facing the neighborhood.

Killing your darlings and making a pivot can be unnerving. It can feel dangerous. But, this sort of pivot brings a single-minded focus and intense commitment to an idea. It's this kind of commitment that brings great rewards.

3. IMAGINING NEW POSSIBILITIES: DON'T BOW TO THE EXPECTATIONS OF OTHERS

There's no noise like the expectations of others, and when you begin to refine your product, offering, or program, you might be met with criticism. You might have a board breathing down your neck, asking why you'd kill a potentially profitable program. You might have community members asking you to chase bigger ideas too soon, to take on more responsibility before you're ready. But if you give in to the expectations of others, you might find yourself back where you started: pursuing too many good things to the exclusion of the best thing.

When refining product offerings, community rebuilding

efforts, or the renewal of any broken system, Refounders imagine how their refounding efforts set them up for future success. They don't allow the noise of others to distract them from their imagination process, either. After all, Refounders know that maintaining the status quo is what created the problem in the first place. They know that forward-thinking imagination produces better results than bending to the tyranny of immediate expectations.

4. CREATING BETTER REALITIES: BREAK YOUR BACK FOR THE ONE CLIENT, PRODUCT, OR IDEA

Refounding is about more than simply imagining. It's about doing—about delivering. Sometimes it's about going above and beyond to deliver better realities for those closest to you.

John Wallace, the people of Bible Center Church, and many of the residents of Homewood have worked hard for their neighborhood. They've treated it like it's the most important place on earth, and though it's not perfect, Homewood is a more beautiful, more flourishing place as a result.

Likewise, we treated our first large customer as if they were the most important in the world. And the truth is, they were, at least for us. We bent over backward for their clinics and caregivers and installed the software in each within the negotiated timeline. And as we continued to work with them over the years, we refined the product more, based on the clinics' needs.

Our refinement, our pivot had put us in a position to win. Still, the question remained: Could we take this success and build on it?

REFOUNDER TAKEAWAYS

- Refounders in complex organizations with complex problems reduce the noise, focusing on solving one problem that might give them momentum.
- Refounders kill their darlings so they can focus on better products, projects, or ideas.
- Refounders will break their back for the client, product, or idea that helps them create a better, more purpose-filled reality.

FIVE

REFOUNDERS MIND THE GAPS

Twenty-seven hospital facilities. It was a lot.

Though our gamble seemed to pay off, we realized that ninety days to install the software might be impossible. Yes, it was SaaS (Software as a Service), but each onsite training took no less than a day and a half, and the clinics were spread out across the country, sometimes in hard-to-reach places, which meant losing time for travel. There were only 64 working days, and New Year's Day fell on a Tuesday, which meant the clinics were closed. Good Friday occurred on the 29th of March, which further narrowed our opportunity to train clinicians. With 27 facilities to train, assuming two days per site, we had 54 installation and training days with 62 calendar opportunities. There was almost no margin of error.

Great with logistics, Chris shined. He sorted out the progression of the installs and we divided up the locations. We made travel plans and developed a client support strategy, which included forwarding calls to each other's cell phones. We had a plan. We could do it.

One of my first trainings was in Anchorage, Alaska. After nearly fifteen hours of travel and a night in a cheap hotel room, I made my way to the hospital, which stood in the shadow of Denali. The team at the hospital was terrific. They were eager to learn and champing at the bit to use the software. As we spoke, they shared their specific needs. The native Inuit people seemed to have a higher incidence of chronic wounds. Why?

It was the first time I'd considered the plight of the patient in earnest. But still, I was more focused on the task at hand. Get the software installed. Move to the next location. Survive, survive, survive.

Sixty-two workdays later, with a few mishaps and lots of airports, the systems were installed and operating. And those early adopters were an absolute godsend. They dove into the software in an attempt to understand it. They questioned it, dissected it, and pointed out the flaws in it. They asked whether we'd considered adding metrics to measure the local oxygen released from capillaries through the skin (what's known as TCPO2 tracking). We were unclear about what TCPO2 was, but they educated us, told us why it was important in wound care. They shared how transcutaneous oxygen monitoring was a great predictor of wound healing. And so, we developed the function.

TCPO2 tracking was just the tip of the iceberg. We were green when it came to wound care. In fact, we knew very little about it. And it turns out that people who knew more than we did about wound care had a lot to say. They explained how functions to track these issues were critical to holistic wound care monitoring, and we implemented their best ideas.

With our first large client installations complete, and with over 10,000 wound assessments now populating our benchmarking, we attempted to expand our footprint. I met with doctors all over the country and in our own backyard. Along the way, I met Dr. David Steed, a vascular surgeon working at the University of Pittsburgh Medical Center. Among wound-care geeks, he is nothing short of a legend, so there's no reason he should have taken a shine to me. Still, he was generous with his time and, understanding the mission we were attempting, he shared about an upcoming conference: the largest gathering of wound care clinicians in the country, and it happened every year. There would be hundreds of doctors and a thousand wound care nurses there, and it might be a great opportunity, he said.

I cold-called the conference organizers, hoping to get my foot in the door. We were a small company, I said, but we were creating software that could help doctors and patients with chronic wound care. We were hoping to find some space to present our software. Pitch made, the woman on the other end of the line said vendors were invited to set up booths during the two-and-a-half days of the convention. It was the perfect opportunity, but there was a catch. It was a few thousand dollars to rent the space, and that didn't include booth design and setup. I reminded her that we were small (though I did not tell her we were near-bankruptcy small), but that our product fit a niche need. They should invite us to attend on some sort of scholarship, I said.

She didn't bite.

I called Chris and pitched him on plan B. I'd fly to Las
Vegas with lots of single-page brochures and business cards.
Even though Net Health wouldn't have a booth, I'd pitch our
system person to person if I had to. I would win friends and
influence people! I would take the wound-care community by
storm, and by the time I left, we'd have scores of new clients.
Right?

Chris wasn't so sure it would work. I pressed hard, convinced him it would. And besides, after all the negotiating and
hustling we'd done, this would be simple. We couldn't miss.
Chris capitulated, and I tapped our thin reserves, dropped
a few hundred dollars on a plane ticket and a few hundred
more on a hotel room. We printed a hundred dollars' worth of
high-resolution flyers with wound care pictures and the name
WoundExpert plastered on the front. And a few short weeks
later, I was on a plane to Sin City.

During the flight, I practiced my pitch and prepared to
overcome all objections. I considered the questions that might
come up and the answers I'd give.

So, how long have you been in business? It's complicated, but
we're a great comeback story.

What do you know about wound care? Not much really, but
we're learning a lot from another client.

How many facilities use your software? Um, almost thirty.

What doctors and nurses did you work with to develop the system?
(Hmmm.)

Are you a software engineer? Um . . . no, but let me tell you
about my partner Chris.

So, why are you here and what do you actually know? (Bow my
head in shame and run for the exit.)

The exercise didn't instill confidence, and my answers were not compelling, but positivity was a strength. Couldn't I fumble my way through explaining what we were all about?

After landing, I couldn't help but smile as I made my way to the convention center. I carried a professional looking laptop bag filled with a stack of amateur-printed brochures and a few hundred business cards. Hospitals, surgical centers, and wound clinics would soon be knocking doors down to work with us, I thought, almost gliding as I walked.

The convention center was buzzing outside, and when I stepped through the doors, I was overcome by the mass of people. There were more than a thousand people milling around, talking with hundreds of vendors. The booths were amazing, some two stories tall, and all of them bright, shiny, and oozing professionalism. Staring down those booths, I wondered what our booth would have looked like had we rented a space. Some PVC booth framing and cardboard signage, hand-lettered with a Sharpie marker? That's about what we could afford, and it would have been a joke compared to these setups.

"Excuse me, I need to see your badge."

I turned and was face-to-face with a security guard.

"Pardon me?"

"I need to see your badge to enter the conference floor."

Badge? I hadn't thought that through.

"I'm here for the conference," I stammered, "and I've flown all the way from Pittsburgh and I'm . . . I'm in the . . . business."

Smooth, Patrick.

"Sir, if you check in over there (pointing to a line of onsite registrars) they will print your badge."

A badge. Easy enough. I thanked him and said, "I'll get that taken care of and be right back."

"What's that?" he asked.

"Never mind. Thanks," I said, and made my way to the check-in station before he had second thoughts about letting me in.

I made my way through the line, all smiles. But at the check-in booth, my nerves fired back up.

"What's your last name?" the worker behind the booth asked.

"Colletti."

"Hmmm. What company are you with?"

"Net Health Systems," I responded, thinking *systems* gave us an air of size and credibility.

"I don't have any companies listed under that name." She looked up from her screen without asking whether it could be under another name or whether I'd like to register on the spot. I was trying to break the ice with a smile. She wasn't having it.

"I am just here to walk the tradeshow floor," I said. "We have a software system for wound care, and I'm trying to get the lay of the land."

"Do you have a tradeshow booth?" she asked.

"No, I'm just here to connect with future partners."

She gave me the raw news. Non-registrants weren't allowed to wander the floor. But there was a silver lining. If I was a certified wound-care clinician, she said, onsite registration was just under a thousand dollars.

I stood there blinking, and all I could manage to say was, "I'm not certified."

She nodded, asked if I was with a larger company, said I might be added to their attendee list for $500. I racked my brain, considered who I might know that wouldn't mind me tagging my name onto their list. No one.

She said she'd talk to her manager and then slinked behind a curtain wall. When she returned, she was smiling. There was a compromise. For $695, they could give me a two-day pass. There was only one problem: I didn't have $695 to spend. I asked if she could reduce the price, since I was only there for 24 hours, which wasn't two days. She looked at me with pity and said $500 was the best she could do.

I'd come all the way from Pittsburgh, had paid for airfare and a hotel room and the truth was, I didn't have $500 to spend, at least, not on this. Our cash flow was reserved for salaries and installs, not impromptu marketing expenses. And if I dropped the coin without connecting with my partners first? Not cool.

"Are you sure you can't make an exception?"

"No sir, sorry. Maybe we'll see you next year?"

Sure thing. If we survived.

I walked through the giant common area, watching all the people go into what was, to me, a veritable amusement park. The security guard made eye contact with me, removing any inkling I had to just sneak in. That look drove the message home. I'd failed. I was a fool. How could I have been so stupid to fly all the way here on a whim and a prayer in an effort to make some magical connections? What's more, I'd wasted money and felt like I made a bad decision with what small amount of working capital we had.

Outside the convention center showroom, I noticed a

group congregating around a giant corkboard wall. Ten feet wide and eight feet high, it was covered with what looked like a giant pile of help-wanted cards. It seemed to be a sort of meetup station for all sorts of people, too. A tacked piece of paper indicated the wound care nurses of Minnesota were meeting there at 7:00 in the morning. There was also a 5K the following morning at 7:30, and all were invited. A scientific team studying diabetic foot ulcers were meeting for coffee the following afternoon at 2:30. As I looked at the messages on the board, it dawned on me that this was their version of an online message board, except it was physical. And it was getting a lot of traffic.

That's when the idea hit me.

When the traffic thinned out for the plenary sessions, I claimed a three-by-three swath of that corkboard space. There they were, our low-resolution, overly shiny, poorly produced brochures, proudly sharing the outcomes of our tracking system, "WoundExpert." In the center of that three-by-three block of brochures was my business card. I stepped back, admired my admittedly corporate art, and imagined it would do the trick.

Full of guerilla-marketing enthusiasm, I moved to the common area tables, where I placed brochures and cards between the chairs meant for casual gatherings. If there was an open space, I threw down my shiny brochures. On those brochures were photos of well-measured wounds, and now those photos were spread around the convention center lobby. You couldn't walk ten feet without seeing the name WoundExpert, the name of our software. It was beautiful, at least as far as open-wound literature can be described as beautiful.

I made my way back to the board, and I noticed a sign with an arrow that read, "Poster presentations this way." It was free to the public, the sign said, so I made my way to the area, and as I entered, I saw people proudly displaying their experiments and studies. It was like an adult science fair, with almost one-third of the posters including their proud researchers. There was a poster on the microbiology of the wound bed. One on tissue dynamics associated with smoking? Diabetes and vascularity? Count me in.

As I read the posters, I started to realize what a complex problem chronic wound care really was. I read how over 100,000 people lose one of their limbs each year due to complications of wounds, particularly people with diabetes. Why? I read about the risks of depression, mortality, and even suicide associated with amputation. But I noticed something curious on many of those posters. They used rulers to measure wound size and low-quality digital cameras to photograph the progression of healing. That's when it dawned on me: We could help them up their game.

I struck up conversations with the poster presenters, and when people asked what I did, I explained the technology, how we were already implementing our system in a handful of clinics across the country. I shared how we could track wound measurements more accurately, how the tool could be indispensable for wound care clinicians. Questions abounded. I generated leads. Our software clicked with these on-the-ground practitioners, even if they picked up on the fact that we had little practical knowledge of the wound-care field.

As I spoke with these medical professionals, a theme emerged. They needed comparative data. If they used our software, I said, they could generate comparative sets. They listened, told me that's exactly what the industry needed. There wasn't a lot of scientific evidence about the norms of wound healing at that time, they said. And over and over, they indicated how this impacted their research on diabetic wound research.

The opportunity to independently benchmark unique healing methods to others was the basis of the scientific method and might be valuable in grant-writing. What's more, millions of people each year required care, and the doctors said this kind of benchmarking might actually change the methods of treatments for those patients.

With each conversation, I became more convinced. There was a gap in wound care treatment, and our software package might go a long way to filling that gap. The product was bigger than a tool for twenty-seven wound-care facilities. In fact, it could be an industry game-changer, even if it was a relatively small industry.

LESSONS FROM THE STRIP

Once a Refounder defines and addresses Problem Zero, once she refines the approach to the simplest, most viable idea, she gets to work identifying solutions. It might be identifying a niche for a refined product. It might be retooling departmental procedures to measure more meaningful information. (More on this in chapter 8, which touches on leading and lagging indicators.) Once the Refounder identifies the potential solution, she commits. And though this is paramount in discrete systems, like businesses, it's important in all contexts, including the municipal context. And this is exactly what Pittsburghers did in the Strip District in the first decade of the 2000s.[15]

The Strip District is one of the most unique districts in all of Pennsylvania. It's a half-mile long, flat "strip" down the heart of Pittsburgh, and it's significantly longer than it is wide. On the northwest, it's bordered by the Allegheny River. To the southeast, it's hemmed in by Pittsburgh's Hill District. It's one of the earliest settlements of the city, and it has quite the history.

Over 250 years ago, the future first president George Washington came to Pittsburgh in the middle of a Pennsylvania winter. It was November of 1753, and the then-twenty-one-year-old major in the Virginia militia had set out to deliver a diplomatic message from the Governor of Virginia to the French at Fort Le Boeuf. The message? *Stay off our land.*

On his return journey at the end of that year—with the weather getting even worse and his horses failing—Washington tried to cross the icy Allegheny on a rudimentary raft with his traveling companion, Christopher Gist. The raft wasn't sturdy enough, though, and Washington wasn't a skilled enough navigator, so the raft capsized. And though the river was ice cold, the two men swam for their lives, ultimately crawling out onto an island near the banks of the Strip District and Lawrenceville.

Years later, in 1814, a couple of Pittsburgh residents named James O'Hara and George Bayard took ownership of the half-mile square of land in Pittsburgh near the place

---

15. "The Strip District: A Place Like No Other," PopularPittsburgh.com (November 24, 2014), https://popularpittsburgh.com/stripdistrict-3/.

.

Washington capsized his raft, and they named it, "Northern Liberties of Pittsburgh." Twenty-three years later, the area became part of Pittsburgh proper, joining as the fifth ward. It was in a strategic, ideal area—right up against the Allegheny River—and it quickly became a center for shipping and industry. Foundries, factories, and mills moved their headquarters to this strip of land, and the city's economic growth became inextricably linked with it.

The district boomed, and the businesses there elevated Pittsburgh as one of the key cities of the industrial revolution. Its factories grew in size. So did the population. Immigrants moved into the area looking for work, and the factories benefitted from the influx of labor. Westinghouse, U.S. Steel, and the H. J. Heinz Company (among others) were all incubated right there in what came to be called the Strip. It's the place where Andrew Carnegie started his iron and steel industries and the place where ALCOA (named the Pittsburgh Reduction Company at the time) began producing aluminum.

Because of its location on the river, the Strip also grew into a hub of wholesale food. Cheese, seafood, and produce were shipped in from all over, and the area remade itself. As industry expanded up and down Pittsburgh's three rivers, the wholesale produce business overtook the Strip.

Like businesses, though, municipal districts have a certain shelf life. Without innovation, change, and advancement, communities lose ground. If they don't create a sense of communal gravity, businesses and people will look for it elsewhere. And unfortunately, the Strip lost its sense of communal gravity, and then three events occurred that would shape the future of the Strip District. First, the Great

Depression set in, which led to significant unemployment and contributed to a popup shanty town being constructed in the heart of the district. It created an atmosphere that was anything but appealing to the business people of Pittsburgh.

And just about the time the effects of the Great Depression were waning, a second round of economic devastation came. After heavy spring rains and massive snowmelt, the waters of the Allegheny rose over twenty feet above flood stage. In what's now known as the St. Patrick's Day Flood of 1936, the Strip found itself underwater. Businesses were shuttered. Some lost everything. Hundreds were injured. Dozens died.

And if there was any thought that the Strip District could recover when the waters receded, a third externality intervened. The wholesale produce that anchored the district was virtually eliminated by the grocery store revolution. The larger stores opted to stop using wholesalers and began negotiating directly with growers. The result? Over the following decade, the wholesale produce business became irrelevant, which laid waste to many merchants in the Strip. For decades after that, the Strip struggled to get a foothold, and by the early 2000s, when we moved into the Strip District, aside from the long-standing ethnic markets and an industrial night club, it was almost dead.

Thankfully, it's nothing like that now. Today, it's a vibrant hub of commerce again. So how did Pittsburgh, and the Strip specifically, rediscover themselves? A few things came together.

As part of the foundation, Carnegie Mellon University, a pioneer in computer science, artificial intelligence, and robotics, was producing an over-abundance of strong, young computer engineers in a time when tech was booming. And though many of those engineers packed their bags and moved to Silicon Valley or other booming tech cities, there was a need for a midwestern tech hub. Some of those students wanted to stay in Pittsburgh, and many leaders of Pittsburgh wanted to see it become a unique and even better version of Silicon Valley for the Midwest and Northeast.

Also, because Carnegie Mellon had virtually invented the field of robotics in the 1980s, developing autonomous vehicle technology over the course of two decades and the engineers with the know-how to build them, many companies exploring the up-and-coming industry began targeting the city. With tight streets laid out in a sort of simple grid, the streets approximated something like New York City. So, Uber's Advanced Technology Group came to Pittsburgh for the talent and moved into the Strip, which spearheads the company's automation efforts. Argo AI (which leads Ford's autonomous vehicle business) made the Strip District their home. Aurora, another driverless car tech company, moved in just outside the Strip District (and recently announced plans to relocate into the neighborhood). What's more, other large and recognizable companies, all of which are household names—Apple's cybersecurity division, Facebook Reality Labs, Netflix, Robert Bosch, Target, and Wombat Security—opened offices in the Strip.

We chose the Strip because of its connection to history, because of its unpretentious uniqueness and beauty. There's nothing stuffy about it. Some of the shopkeepers have been there for generations and have weathered the Strip's ups and downs—bakers, butchers, a few shops selling Yinzer gear.[16] Many of those old-school shop owners hose off their storefronts

---

16. "Yinzer" is a colloquialism used to refer to the working-class people of Pittsburgh.

every morning, giving the whole place an open-air, sort of old-world market feel, perfect for a start-up. The price for the office space wasn't bad either. At around $10 per square foot, the space was cheaper than in most parts of the country. And many of our investors and board members worked downtown, so it gave us enough distance to breathe, but put us close enough to walk to a coffee shop or restaurant to meet up.

Throughout the 2000s, the Strip District has been completely revamped. Today, it has some of the best restaurants and coffee shops in Pittsburgh. Its loft apartments house some of Pittsburgh's most famous residents—Steelers, Pirates, and the occasional actor visiting for a movie shoot. There's no doubt about it, the Strip District is where the cool kids hang.

The Strip has new life, and it's in no small part because Pittsburgh innovators examined the landscape and saw the gaps. There was opportunity. There was infrastructure. There was a need. The perfect place existed to create a tech hub, though it would take some refounding. But that's exactly what happened. The city's industry and leadership took something that was broken and made something better. And as person after person stepped into the Strip District gap, the area was refounded and continues to be refounded to this day. Now, the Strip District is a world-renowned center of innovation.

REFOUNDERS MIND THE GAPS

We were made for the Strip District, or the Strip District was made for us; I'm not sure which. But like so many other Pittsburghers we took a bold risk when we relocated to the Strip. And it was that risk tolerance that led me to a conference where I knew no one, had not registered, and had very little plan of attack. And when I discovered I'd attended a conference that was little more than a dead end, I didn't let temporary failure get me down, either. Instead, I looked for an opening, a place I might get a win. And to quote Peter Sims, author of *Little Bets*, "Once a small win has been accomplished, forces are set in motion that favor another small win."

Over the next few years, Net Health reaped the rewards from that one conference and the relationships that Chris helped substantiate through developing stability in the product. We performed hundreds of demonstrations for people who expressed an interest in learning more. We began signing more contracts, scheduling onsite training, and hiring great people. We were pushing new ideas into the software, and our feedback loop from our customers was fast. When lacking the industry bona fides, we relied on and leveraged the strengths of our customers. And slowly but surely, a smart product roadmap emerged.

We pursued our clients' needs with single-minded intensity. We noted where we were and where we needed to be. We followed potential leads and responded to the market. We modified our approach and our product, and eventually we experienced the results. We were agile, growth-oriented, and audacious. We placed bets and earned our wins, which led to other opportunities to win.

Refounders identify the gaps and place bets on their futures. How?

1. TAKE A SOBER LOOK: IDENTIFY YOUR INVENTORY

Before any Refounder can identify the places of his unique potential contribution, he must take a sober look at his inventory of assets. Do you have an amazing product, incredible people (or both)? Do you have a unique approach to problem-solving, a specialized skill? Do you have a refined product or an infrastructure that sets you up for success (like the Strip District did)?

Write down your assets, your skills, your infrastructure, the places where you might be uniquely qualified to meet a need. If it helps, make it visual and draw or sketch it out to see the connections.

2. REFOUNDER'S FOCUS: IDENTIFY THE SOLUTIONS ONLY YOU CAN OFFER

Once you've inventoried your unique assets, examine the gaps in your industry, the market, or the world around you. Identify the solutions you're uniquely equipped to offer. Focus on those solutions. Invest in them. Build coalitions around them.

By attending the wound care conference, I discovered the industry needed a better way to measure healing. Recognizing that need, our team focused on the gap in the industry and worked tirelessly to create the perfect solution. Likewise, knowing the Midwest could use its own tech hub, forward-thinking business leaders in Pittsburgh saw how the city might serve as that hub. Pittsburgh had the right infrastructure (the Strip District), the right educational facilities, and the right people (brilliant computer engineers, software developers, and business minds). And today, it's one of the robotics capitals of the world.

3. IMAGINING NEW POSSIBILITIES: REFOUNDERS SHAPE REALITY

Assets without imagination grow stale. In the same way, focus without imagination will grow stale. With an understanding of their unique assets and solutions only they can offer, bold Refounders imagine better futures and their place in it. Finding the gap they're uniquely equipped to fill, Refounders take the time to see what ought to be and how they fit into that future.

And what happens when we apply our imaginations to the future? In their article for the *Harvard Business Review*, "We Need Imagination Now More Than Ever," Martin Reeves and Jack Fuller write: "With imagination, we can do better than merely adapting to a new environment—we can thrive by shaping it." Applying this notion to the context of the pandemic crisis, they wrote:

In the current COVID-19 crisis, for example:

- The initial emphasis is on rapid **reaction** and defense.
- Then the focus shifts to constructing and implementing plans to endure the likely economic **recession** to follow.
- As the recession abates, the focus shifts to **rebound**—making adjustments to portfolios and channels as we seek to exploit recovering demand.
- Over time the situation becomes more malleable, and imaginative companies shift their focus to **reinventing**—seeking opportunity in adversity by applying more creative approaches to strategy.[17]

---

17. Martin Reeves and Jack Fuller, "We Need Imagination Now More Than Ever," *Harvard Business Review* (April 10, 2020), https://hbr.org/2020/04/we-need-imagination-now-more-than-ever.

Though the emphasis was found in the original text of their article, did you notice the bold word in the final bullet point? Reinventing. Sounds a lot like refounding, doesn't it? Imagination is critical to the refounding process. Refounders see their potential place in the future, and they develop creative solutions to secure that place.

4. CREATING BETTER REALITIES: DON'T HEDGE YOUR BETS

Refounders don't hedge bets. They go all-in, making bold moves that set them up for future success. That's what we did. That's what Pittsburghers did with the Strip District. In fact, it's what all the characters already discussed in this book do. Astro Teller, John Wallace, Josh Armstrong, and the others you'll meet in this book aren't singularly focused on the problem of the day. Instead, they look to the future they want to create, and they sacrifice to create that future.

In the months following the conference, our bet was beginning to pay off. We were adding customers by the day. Business was expanding. We were having more fun. Still, we were playing small ball. We were hitting singles and doubles, advancing runners, scoring runs. But had we identified a clear win for the company outside of profitability? Did we know the purpose of our game? We didn't, but that was all about to change.

REFOUNDER TAKEAWAYS

- Refounders inventory their assets to better understand the solutions only they can offer.
- Refounders see their potential place in the future, and they develop creative solutions to secure their place in it.
- Refounders make bold moves that set them up for future success.

SIX

WORK TOWARD BIGGER PURPOSES

With lower overhead, a refined product, and a customer who needed us as much as we needed them, we were firing on all cylinders, and it was good. The team was growing, the software was humming, and we were growing by the day. And while we certainly had bugs to work out, the feedback we were getting from our clients confirmed we were on the right path. The nurses and caregivers said it was making their lives easier.

If the story ended here, it might sound like any other business success story you've ever read: business nearly fails; team steps in and steps up; team introduces new concepts and ways of doing business; business booms; people win awards and everyone grows wealthy beyond their wildest dreams—the end. Except that's not where the story ended. Really, it was where the story began, because while I was on a software install at one of those first clinics, I met someone who changed my life: Lenora.

Before I met Lenora, my focus was on one thing: turning the company around. But was it infused with any purpose other than turning a profit or simply not failing? Not really. And the truth was, I hadn't thought twice about anything *but* having a business success story. Serving clients, creating a positive culture—these were all just the right thing to do, but ultimately for me a means to an end. I believed that if you served clients and created a great culture, your company would reap rewards. And the rewards were all I cared about in the early days. But that was about to change.

I'd flown to New Orleans for a new install and decided I'd make an impromptu stop by an existing clinic. It was a practice Chris and I had adopted, traveling to visit existing clients when we were in the region. It was a way to show some love to our customers and build loyalty. It gave us a chance to sit down and listen, too, to get a little inside feedback on what was working and what wasn't. And inevitably, these impromptu visits turned into facility tours. If they had a hyperbaric chamber, they'd regale us with stories of how it helped improve healing for certain wound types. Pure oxygen was pumped in, they said, and once pressurized, that oxygen was pushed into open wounds. And somehow, that combination of pressure and oxygen sped up the healing process. And they were tracking the progress by using our software package.

I loved these tours, but I'd never spent any real time with a patient face-to-face. But on that visit, the program director asked me if I'd like to attend a patient treatment with her. It was the perfect opportunity to see our software in action, she said. So, after signing an additional HIPAA disclosure, I was ready.

Or, so I thought.

Lenora was a warm and welcoming patient, a Black woman in her early sixties. She was being treated for a diabetic wound on her foot. I knew the stats: somewhere around 15–25 percent of people with diabetes will develop lower extremity wounds at some point in their life; 20 percent of diabetics will have one leg amputated; of those with one amputation, 50 percent will have the second leg amputated within five years. Statistics, though, did not convey the human reality. As I looked at Lenora, I could finally put a human face to the problem.

She offered a warm welcome and a broad smile. I asked her to share about her life. She was married with children, she said, and had recently become a grandparent. Hailing from the South, she preferred sweet tea over unsweet and believed politeness was next to only godliness. She had a handful of children and a new grandbaby. There were things to live for.

As she shared, I noticed a large bandage on her foot. There was an odor that could only be classified as sickly floral, one I chalked up to a combination of her growing wound, the antiseptic used to treat it, and the strong cleaners used to sterilize the room. The room itself was spotless and basic, and beside Lenora's bed, the patient-monitoring software was up and running. After asking permission, I read the notes and saw she'd been in treatment for more than a month at this wound clinic. But that wasn't the concerning thing. I stared at the screen, thinking I couldn't be reading it right. She'd been suffering from the same wound for over two years? Was such a thing possible?

It turns out that she, like hundreds of thousands of others suffering from chronic wounds, had bounced around from primary care physician to specialist then back to a variety of other well-meaning people. Some didn't understand the seriousness of the wound and likely didn't believe it would ever be healed. I pointed to the screen, then turned to the program director.

"Two years?"

Without a word, she nodded. Some well-meaning doctors tried to help, she said, but they couldn't get the wound to close up. That's why she was here, Lenora said, just as the doctor entered with the nurse.

He welcomed Lenora, then turned and shook my hand. Smiling, he mentioned that I must be with the "computer people," then turned to the nurse, who was already unwrapping the bandages on Lenora's foot. Fully exposed, I noted the gravity of the situation. There, wrapped around her foot was a wound the size of a plum. It varied in color across the wound, yellowish on the outside and deep red at the center. Those yellowish edges were dry and scaly, but the red patches were oozy. Within moments of the bandage coming off, the room was filled with the pungent, profound smell that no room cleaner or air freshener could cover up.

She was in a tender situation, and her eyes darted around the room, looking for a reassuring glance. I looked down, then back at the chart, avoiding eye contact and the overwhelming desire to tell her everything was okay. After all, it wasn't. Was it?

The doctor asked questions and she answered. She walked with a limp and was embarrassed to have her dressings changed at home. She thought her family avoided her because of the smell of the wound. The pain was one thing, she said, but the distance her wound created between her and her family was another. The embarrassment was another, still. She didn't want her grandbaby to think she was a beast.

"I just keep thinking it will heal," she said, "but each doctor tries something new, and nothing seems to work. Maybe my body is no good at healing anymore."

With a straight face, her doctor reassured her. It wasn't that her body *couldn't* heal, it was just that her underlying health condition made the healing more difficult. Diabetes led to poor circulation, he said, and poor circulation made it difficult for her white blood cells to do the healing work. Recurring bacterial infection further complicated things. But she could give her body a fighting chance if she took control of her health. She needed to refrain from cigarettes and sweet tea, needed to eat plenty of protein and follow the off-loading and dressing change regime she'd started a month ago. No matter how much it smelled or how embarrassing it was, he said, she had to change the bandage. She had to do what it took so that she could close the distance between her and her support system. She had to do what it took so that she wouldn't ultimately lose her foot to amputation. Would she commit?

I could tell she wanted to believe, but she had gotten her hopes up before. Why should it be any different now? Then she asked the question I'd been wondering myself: Why should she give up smoking and tea if she wasn't seeing any progress?

The doctor did his best to coax a commitment to a healthy lifestyle, telling her to trust the process. All the while, the nurse continued with her assessment. She measured the wound from all directions and put the information into the software system we'd created. And after it was measured, the doctor pulled a cart carrying a tray of surgical tools toward him. "Now we'll debride the wound," he said, using a scalpel to slice away the dry and scaly skin at the margins. As fresh blood arrived, the nurse wiped it away. And what emerged when they were finished was something that approximated a larger, though somewhat cleaner wound.

Why would they make the wound larger?

I wanted to encourage Lenora, tell her everything looked great. Except I didn't have the expertise to make that kind of a call. So, I watched and tried to continue looking positive, though, to be honest, I still couldn't figure out why it was a good idea to make the wound bigger. Shouldn't we be trying to close it up?

There were more measurements, more inputs into the computer. The nurse printed out a report, then showed it to the doctor and Lenora with a smile. "Look at the line showing your volume change. If you look at the time-series analysis of photos and measurements, you can see that the volume has shrunk by 35 percent in seven weeks. That means your body is working!"

Lenora's cheeks began to dimple and a small smile crept onto her face. "This is me?" she asked, pointing at the charts and graphs. "Yes," the nurse continued. "Your wound is getting smaller, despite the appearance that it's getting larger. Within two months it should be completely closed up."

"But they said I might lose my leg this time," Lenora said tentatively, in a quiet voice.

"Not if we have anything to do with it," the doctor assured her, "and not if you do what it takes to keep your body working."

Lenora asked to keep the printout, and the doctor said it was fine. She took it, and she stared at the line of progress. In that moment, my life became richer. It was patient engagement 1.0.

We walked from the room, and the program director said when patients with chronic wounds don't have a reason to believe, they often give up. They become depressed. Often, they turn back to smoking, drinking, eating unhealthily, because if their body isn't going to cooperate in the healing process, they might as well enjoy what life they have left.

"Frequently, it ends in amputation before the patient has ever made it to a wound care facility," she said. "But if we can reassure them that their body hasn't turned against them, that caring for their body will lead to the right results, we think more of our patients will start to see big wins. Just like Lenora did today."

I thanked her for letting me spend time with Lenora and told her I'd be processing the moment for a long time. As I left, I considered how many times I'd heard parents say that the birth of a child expanded their capacity to love and their purpose in life, all in a matter of moments. That day, I felt something similar. Whereas I'd been hyper-focused on success, the experience in the clinic opened my eyes to the true purpose of our business—giving caregivers the tools they needed to make measurable differences in the lives of their patients.

I'm embarrassed to say that before that moment, I was pretty myopic and maybe more than a little self-centered. The idea of turning around a dot-com company, of pulling off some great corporate rags-to-riches story, was my main motivation. But in just twenty minutes, I'd witnessed how those caregivers were changing the course of Lenora's life in a meaningful, measurable way. They'd given her hope that she might have a normal life, a life without the distance from her family, without the guilt, shame, or pain that accompanied her wounded leg. They'd given her a purpose, too, a reason to keep pursuing healing. What's more, they'd used our software to do it. And when she held our report, she'd been engaged. Our code, our effort, and our work touched Lenora. And as a result, I was touched too.

Our software?

What we were doing was so much bigger than I'd realized. We were offering a tool doctors and nurses could use to bring healing to a leg, a psyche, and even a family. That was a big purpose, a purpose worth pursuing.

REFOUNDERS WANTED: A HEALTHCARE CRISIS

Lenora changed my life and the direction of our company, and since meeting her, I've done my part to learn more about chronic wounds, particularly those related to diabetic conditions.

In medical circles, a chronic wound is one which doesn't heal in thirty days or less. Anyone can suffer from these kinds of wounds—cancer survivors, those with compromised immune systems, patients suffering from vascular problems. The condition is most commonly seen in the most vulnerable populations, though—the elderly in nursing homes, diabetics without access to proper medical care, and people of color. And as every American knows, the American medical care system doesn't always work best for the most vulnerable populations. And when they slip through the cracks, the results can be devastating.

Diabetes—a disease marked by high blood sugar levels caused by the body's failure to produce insulin—wreaks havoc on the body. Diabetic patients have a 15–25 percent chance of developing diabetic foot ulcers. Between 10 and 15 percent of these ulcers do not heal, and of those, 25 percent will lead to an amputation. Even worse, of those who suffer an amputation, up to 40 percent will die within two years. But according to medical experts, "The risk for amputation may be decreased by up to 75 percent if a team specializing in the care of diabetic foot ulcers is involved. This team may consist of specialists in wound care, diabetic podiatry, infectious disease, and a vascular specialist."[18] And because of the work Net Health does in chronic wound care, I know one of the preeminent surgeons taking just this kind of team approach.

If I were creating my own rock and roll hall of fame, my first inductee (aside from my mother) would be Eddie Vedder. My second pick would be Dr. David Armstrong, professor of surgery at the Keck School of Medicine at the University of Southern California, who specializes in amputation prevention. As the founder of the Southwestern Academic Limb Salvage Alliance (SALSA), he's a bit of a living legend in chronic-wound treatment circles, and lest you think my classification of him as a rock star is a bit far-fetched, as of the writing of this book, Dr. Armstrong's wailing rendition of AC/DC's "You Shook Me All Night Long" can be found on YouTube.

I met Dr. Armstrong years ago through my work, and I've

---

18. "25 MUST-Know Statistics about Amputation Due to Diabetes," Azura Vascular Care (April 11, 2017), https://www.azuravascularcare.com/infopad/diabetic-foot-amputation-stats/.

heard his spiel a dozen times, the salient points of which are as follows: 34 million Americans suffer from diabetes; of those, almost one-half suffer from diabetic-induced nerve damage of the hands and feet; because of the nerve damage, patients lose what Dr. Armstrong calls "the gift of pain"; without pain, tiny pressure ulcers form, widen, and become full-on diabetic wounds; those wounds often putrefy, become smelly and infected. The result? By the time patients enter treatment, surgeons are left with little choice but to amputate. In fact, there's a diabetic amputation every twenty seconds.

Dr. Armstrong has devoted his entire career to reducing the number of diabetic amputations. Why? I wanted to drill to the bottom of that question, so I called Dr. Armstrong and we discussed and debated: Why would a doctor who could have excelled in any surgical field specialize in podiatric surgery on the diabetic foot?

He chuckled, hemmed and hawed about it being in his blood (his father was a podiatrist), but then he offered a leveling answer. "Those with diabetic wounds are the lepers of our day. They're overlooked and often uncared for. So, it is my honor to treat them." He could have left it at that, busy as he was, having just come from surgery. He didn't, though. Instead, he offered a story.

After medical school, the young Dr. Armstrong was offered an elite surgical residency at the Kern Hospital for Special Surgery in Detroit. There, he'd had his own epiphany, an experience that set the course of his career. He'd assisted in reconstructive surgery on the foot of a famous college basketball player, a giant of a man. While making the rounds the following day, he stopped by the patient's room for a routine post-op visit. After examining the surgical wound, changing the dressing, and asking about his pain, which was significant, Dr. Armstrong made his way back out to the hallway. There, he caught a glimpse of a woman in the neighboring room, and what he saw pulled him in.

She was a tiny woman, an immigrant with a large group of family members gathered around her bed. She had a large wound on her foot that hadn't yet been treated. There was dead tissue around the edges of the wound, and it needed to be removed if the wound was going to heal. Dr. Armstrong asked whether he could tend to it, and through her son who was interpreting, she agreed.

He set to work debriding the wound, and while he did, he noticed the ends of the woman's fingers were missing. He pointed, asked her what happened, and the wispy woman told him she was a baker. Over the years of making naan in a scorching hot tandoor—a cylindrical clay oven—she'd seared her fingers off. But it wasn't just the heat alone that led to the loss of her fingers. She suffered from both diabetes and leprosy, which led to the loss of feeling in her fingertips. Without feeling, she never realized she was burning her fingers down to the nub.

The woman didn't wince once as Dr. Armstrong worked on her foot. When he was finished, she thanked him. And as he walked out of her room, he considered his options. Yes, performing reconstructive surgeries (particularly for athletes) was sexy, perhaps lucrative. But treating chronic foot wounds was something different. He sensed personal purpose in helping those in the margins, the "the modern-day lepers," and so, he knew what he had to do. He chose the road less taken. He's been focused on treating foot wounds ever since.

It was a fortuitous decision. Over the following two decades, he'd watch as the percentage of Americans with diabetes skyrocketed. But according to Dr. Armstrong, the doctors who've treated the wounds associated with diabetes often fail to take a holistic view of the patient. For many, their first inclination is to amputate the infected area. Why? Removing the appendage keeps the infection from spreading, leading to even further complications. Still, it's a short-sighted approach, according to Dr. Armstrong.

"This is about more than treating the hole in the person. It's about treating the whole person," he said. Pressing the issue, I asked him what he meant, and that's when he gave me the unfiltered version. The medical system doesn't always work the way it should, he said. It doesn't incentivize cross-disciplinary approaches. Nowhere is that more important than in the field of diabetic wound treatment, where amputations are often recommended as the primary course of treatment.

I ask how his approach differs, and Dr. Armstrong shares how he's taken a multidisciplinary approach to diabetic foot care in an effort to stop willy-nilly amputations. Taking a "toe and flow" approach, Dr. Armstrong doesn't simply treat the wound (or amputate the appendage). Instead, he brings in a team of specialists. At the center of the team is a podiatrist who examines the foot (the "toe" portion of the approach) and a vascular surgeon who determines whether surgery might increase the blood flow to an infected area (the "flow" portion of the approach), which jumpstarts healing. He involves behavioral health experts who challenge the patient to change their lifestyle habits, including their diet and exercise regimens. He includes mental health professionals in the mix, who help the patients overcome depression and feelings of isolation. And if insurance won't foot the bill (pun intended), Dr. Armstrong offsets the costs from clinic profits. This, he says, creates a better, more sustainable method for achieving his big purpose—fewer amputations.

There are too many factors and too few medical specialists working together to bring real solutions to those who suffer from diabetic foot wounds, and the stakes are too high. And fueled by the bigger purpose of his epiphany—caring for the overlooked, those in the margins—Dr. Armstrong has taken a Refounders approach. He noticed the deficiencies in the system and filled them. The result?

The "toe and flow" model is working. This team-based approach is showing marked reduction in amputations relating to diabetic foot wounds. He points to a test case, a hospital in Calgary that implemented this model. When compared with Edmonton, where the model wasn't implemented, Calgary enjoyed a 45 percent lower rate of major amputations.[19]

REFOUNDERS ARE FUELED BY PURPOSE

Dr. Armstrong is fueled by purpose, and it has made all the difference in his work. And over the years, I've had the privilege of meeting so many healthcare workers—doctors, nurses, and technicians—just like him. They put a face with their purpose, and it drives what they do. But in those early refounding

---

19. R. Basiri, B. D. Haverstock, P. F. Petrasek, and K. Manji, "Reduction in Diabetes-Related Major Amputation Rates After Implementation of a Multidisciplinary Model: An Evaluation in Alberta, Canada," *Journal of the American Podiatric Medicine Association* (online) (November 1, 2019), https://europepmc.org/article/med/31674800.

days, Chris and I were focused on surviving, on meeting a sprinter's goal.

Reduce debt.

Increase sales.

Develop needed functionality.

That's not all bad, of course. These are the kinds of goals that keep you alive, but are they enough to keep you going for the long haul? Are they the kinds of goals that can fuel a purpose-driven business that will make an impact on society? I don't know, and I'm grateful I didn't have to find out. I'm grateful I met Lenora, that I saw her wound, that I experienced her relief when she discovered her body was not against her and that she could play a role in her own healing. Lenora's relief, the hope she experienced when she saw the pictorial and graphical view from our software, made its way to my heart. That changed everything.

I've been a part of a Refounders story, and I've had the privilege of walking with other Refounders. Through those stories, I've learned this simple truth: True Refounders operate from purposes bigger than profit.

In his book *The Infinite Game*, Simon Sinek expands on this idea. He writes that a successful venture should not focus on finite goals—i.e., profits, EBITDA, gross sales—but instead, should focus on the infinite, a "Just Cause." A Just Cause, he writes, "is a specific vision of a future state that does not yet exist; a future state so appealing that people are willing to make sacrifices in order to help advance toward that vision." What's the effect of adopting a Just Cause? Sinek puts it this way:

. . . [W]hen there is a Just Cause, a reason
to come to work that is bigger than any particular win, our days take on more meaning
and feel more fulfilling. Feelings that carry on
week after week, month after month, year after year. In an organization that is only driven
by the finite, we may like our jobs some days,
but we will likely never *love* our jobs. If we
work for an organization with a Just Cause,
we may like our jobs some days, but we will
always love our jobs.[20]

I know this to be true. It's been almost twenty years since
my interaction with Lenora, and I think about her regularly. On
the days when the business feels messy, or there's a seemingly
unsolvable problem to solve, I remember Lenora, together with
the millions of patients who need help, care, and love. This
purpose—or as Sinek calls it, my "Just Cause"—motivates me.

If you find yourself refounding only around the idea of
increasing profits, stop now. Go back to the drawing board.
Ask yourself these bigger purpose questions. When you identify that purpose, pursue it relentlessly.

1. TAKE A SOBER LOOK: WHAT BREAKS YOUR HEART ABOUT THE WORLD?

We do not live in a perfect world. We live in a world that's
often chaotic, fractured, and broken. And what's true of the
world may be true of your business, your neighborhood, your

---

20. Simon Sinek, *The Infinite Game* (New York: Penguin, 2019), 32–33.

community of faith, or even your marriage. If you're a true Refounder, these things break your heart. By taking a sober look at the things that break your heart and the particular gifts or skills you can apply (of the products or skills of your company), you might identify a bigger purpose to serve.

2. REFOUNDER'S FOCUS: CAN I PUT A PARTICULAR NAME OR FACE TO MY PURPOSE?

When you're honing your bigger purpose, focus on a particular person. Why? Because when purposes become personal, they become actionable. You begin to work toward good things for that person.

When I met Lenora, I could put a face to the bigger purpose of Net Health. We weren't just serving nameless patients spread out across America. We were serving actual people. And when I went into the office each day, Lenora's face motivated me to do the best work I could do. She became emblematic of my bigger purpose.

3. IMAGINING NEW POSSIBILITIES: WHAT DECISION CAN I MAKE TODAY TO PUT PURPOSE FIRST?

Putting your purpose first doesn't happen by accident. Instead, pursuing your purpose takes intention. So, each day, imagine one decision you can make to prioritize your bigger purpose. If you have to, carve out ten minutes at the beginning of each day and imagine ways to pursue your purpose.

And for the record, this does not mean that you won't imagine ways to increase profits. In fact, it can be quite to the contrary in business. I was motivated to make the best decisions I could make, to increase earnings so we could serve more people just like Lenora. So, day after day I went into the office imagining potential decisions I could make that might make her life just a little bit better. If it meant scheduling a call with a nurse in order to understand how to make our software incrementally better, I'd do it. If it meant hiring a bigger sales team to get our software to market, I'd schedule interviews. Whatever the task, if it served our bigger purpose, I'd commit to it.

4. CREATING BETTER REALTIES: HOW WILL I KNOW WHEN I'M PURPOSE-FOCUSED?

When you're focused on your bigger purpose, the natural outcome will be better realities for the people in the world around you. So, to understand whether you're purpose-focused, ask yourself: Are lives better off because of my work in the world?

Take some time and create a list of outcomes that would indicate whether you're creating the kind of purpose-directed outcomes you want in the world. Keep it handy and refer to it often. Aim to produce those outcomes. And when you start seeing them come to fruition, you'll know you're on track.

As we heard more and more stories like Lenora's, I knew we were focused on our bigger purpose. What's more, as our team members began to hear these stories, I noted how much more willing they were to sacrifice for our clients and their patients. It was a sure sign. We were a purpose-oriented company.

Consider each of the above questions. Write the answers to these questions where you'll see them every day. Return to them often. When you get distracted by profits, when you find yourself chasing them like a dog chases its tail, stop. Return to your purpose. Ask what you'll *do* with your profits to advance your ultimate purpose. If you can't answer that question, start back with question one and work your way forward.

As we began chasing our bigger purpose, we began to realize it was too limited. Yes, the patients we served were priority number one. But if we wanted the best solutions for our clients, we'd need to get the best out of our employees. How could we get the best out of our employees if we didn't create a culture of success? If our people didn't enjoy work, wouldn't that be reflected in the product?

An audacious idea began to take hold. Perhaps our bigger purpose wasn't just limited to the patients we serve. Perhaps it was about all the people. Maybe we could use capitalism to change the lives of patients, clients, and the people who walked the halls of our office every day. And when this broader vision of purpose took hold, we doubled down. In fact, we put our money where our mouths were.

REFOUNDER TAKEAWAYS

- Refounders examine what breaks their heart in the world, then they set out to solve it.
- Refounders have a purpose bigger than profits, and they pursue it relentlessly.
- Refounders always, always, always put purpose first.

SEVEN

REINVEST IN BIGGER PURPOSES

I got it. I understood the real power of our platform, how it could change the lives of real people in real pain. If we could provide a tool that brought the hope of healing to Lenora, we could cast a wider net and help others. It was a clarified purpose; it wasn't about us. With it, we refined our software demonstration. It was a 60-minute symphony, an early pitch deck sharing the future of wound healing and the sophistication our software brought to it. I traveled the country, shared it with all who would listen. It was a compelling story, and as I shared it, our footprint began to grow.

It wasn't just our footprint that grew, either. Our talent expanded. We hired Mike, a brash young guy who'd been trained to sell stocks in New York. He'd moved back to Pittsburgh after 9/11 and was focused on starting a life away from the chaos of Manhattan. A born storyteller and a quick study, Mike learned our product quickly and had an easy way with clients. Unfortunately, he was prone to fainting at the sight of any wound care photos, but we made it work. He became the anchor of our sales team.

Our technology team was starting to click, too. Chris found two key developers—Vinay and Kyle—each of whom brought different skills to the table. Along with his development capabilities, Vinay had an infectious enthusiasm and interest in doing what it took to help our clients succeed. He'd answer midnight calls in an effort to troubleshoot issues from our West Coast clients and would drop everything to drive to any client location within a few hundred miles if it meant providing better service. Kyle was more focused on the future, focusing on successfully bundling the day's business needs with a long-term view of our software's architecture. He was the catalyst behind our continuous improvement approach, always making sure that we were better prepared for tomorrow's work. Together, these key employees fueled our entrepreneurial spirit while ensuring we were built to last.

The team was coming together, and the financial trend lines were aimed in the right direction—up and to the right. We were quickly becoming a viable company, and Chris and I could see just far enough down the line to imagine possibilities. If we could build a thriving team, we could scale the company. If we could scale the company, we'd increase earnings. And if we increased the earnings, we could double down on a key focus area: creating an amazing corporate culture that excited our teammates and set an example of community for our peers. It was a virtuous cycle, at least as we saw it.

As our sales and marketing team grew—we were seven strong—I turned over much of the day-to-day management for software demonstrations, hoping the team we'd brought together would flourish. And they did. As one quarter passed to the next, we were beginning to feel the "flywheel effect," a concept outlined by Jim Collins in his book *Good to Great.* By making one right decision at a time, it was as if we were pushing a giant flywheel, and with each turn of that wheel, we were building unstoppable momentum. The sales team was scheduling demos. Existing customers were recommending us to their peers. We implemented an advisory board. We began closing sales and adding customers on a weekly basis. We were onboarding clients, and as they provided feedback, we refined the product. The result? We were doubling in size every fifteen months.

The industry started to take notice. What's more, the city began to take notice. Within three years of our refounding we were awarded the Tech 50 award for the fastest growing tech company in Pittsburgh. We were quickly becoming an important player in our hometown, an anchor tenant of the growing Strip District. And we were having a blast doing it.

Still, it wasn't all smooth sailing. And as Phife (rest in peace) from A Tribe Called Quest said, "I never let a statue tell me how nice I am."[21] And what's true of the rap game is just as true in corporate America.

With our fast and sustained growth, the early investors and former board members started coming out of the woodwork. They pulled chairs up to the table with varying requests, ideas, and demands. Some thought we should scale back our hiring, grow more slowly, and distribute dividends. Some thought we

---

21. A Tribe Called Quest, "Award Tour," from *Midnight Marauders,* Jive Records, 1993.

should reinvest every penny we'd earned in an effort to grow faster. Others thought we should diversify, switch business models, or invest in products that were a little sexier. One thought we should essentially bet the company on a product that would produce "hockey stick growth" in a hardware solution that was a longshot. A few went so far as to say we should sell the entire company. The truth? All of these opinions were valid, at least from a business perspective.

Still, Chris and I—together with Anthony, who had continued to be the most constructive board member and served as the chairman of the board—had a clear line of sight. We were bullish on all things Net Health, and our strategy had paid off. We thought it best to stay the course. In fact, Chris and I believed that within a few more years we'd push $10 million a year in recurring revenue with plentiful margins, and we would consider other products. We were at an important inflection point. While the vast majority of start-ups never reach $2 million in revenue, if we could crest $10 million with strong margins, we could become our own platform and add other products. In other words, diversifying now was the wrong play. If anything, we needed to dig deeper into the field of chronic wound care, even if some sexier diversification strategy presented itself.

We were laser-focused, making moves straight out of the Refounder's playbook. Now, we were reaping the rewards. Sales were increasing. Our cash reserves were growing. Still, I listened to all sides and did my best to navigate the differences of opinion (and some downright dissension). As I did, I began to synthesize what was really happening. We had come through a dramatic season. On the verge of folding, with little or no prospect of sales, many of these investors thought they'd lost everything. And now that the getting was good, some wanted recognition and return for that drama. Some wanted to get out before Net Health experienced another downturn, but the truth was, no one was willing to say it. And so, urgency and a lack of trust set in amongst shareholders and the board members.

I considered the direction the dissatisfied shareholders hoped to push us, and the truth set in—they'd never be satisfied with our work. So, Anthony, Chris, and I met in a local coffee shop and considered our options. Did we think our growth pattern was sustainable? Yes. Were we confident in our strategy for the future? Absolutely. Was there still potential to grow the business and then turn to untapped markets? Could we continue to create a community that embodied the early mantra: "We are here to grow personally, professionally, and in our community"? We had no doubt. There was a solid consensus among Anthony, Chris, and me. We'd not yet seen the full potential of this company or its opportunities, and we wanted to stay the course.

We took time to develop a thoughtful shareholder letter and sent out a notice. We'd hold the annual meeting of our dysfunctional shareholder family, where we'd deliver our analysis of the future. No sooner had the letters gone out, information requests started flying. Board members requested copies of the capitalization table showing who owned what amount of stock. They asked for forms for proxy voting. (A proxy, simply put, is the right of one shareholder to vote for another.) We knew what this meant: a battle was brewing. A coalition of shareholders was amassing, and we knew what they wanted. They intended to try and either force a sale or fire the existing board and take another unknown strategy. And though there was no doubt we could sell our growing company and realize a pretty good return, it would be a mistake. In a few years, we could be a thriving example of how great culture refines capitalism. And, of equal importance, we could continue exploring ideas we had about modern management and culture-building, many of which were incredible enough with 50 teammates but would be extraordinary if we could grow to a connected community of 1,000 or more teammates.

The day of the meeting came, and Anthony, Chris, and I were well-rehearsed and as prepared as we could be. Shareholders arrived and nervous chatter began. Some gathered in the oversized boardroom, pulled out their calculators, put on their glasses, and prepared for battle. Shoulders drew up around the ears. The walls seemed to press in.

Anthony called the meeting to order and after a brief introduction, he turned it over to Chris and me for operating updates. It was easy enough to deliver, given that we had grown by 50 percent a year (or more) for five consecutive years. We had actual earnings. We had cash savings. We'd expanded our software package—WoundExpert—and were gaining notoriety in the healthcare world, too. But, no one seemed to be listening. Instead everyone seemed to be planning for what would come next—the annual voting for the slate of directors.

It was the directors who could force the issue of the sale.

It was the shareholders who voted for the directors.

It became apparent that two groups were emerging, each plotting a takeover of the board. The groups cordoned themselves into separate board rooms, and I went between both, trying to answer questions and build a bridge. I tried to develop a compromise that would preserve the course of the company, but there was none to be had.

The dissenting shareholders had made a tactical mistake, and we knew it. They'd overplayed their hand. Had they simply chosen to elect a board who would force a distribution of dividends, perhaps they could have gathered enough votes. But platforming potential board members who would sell the entire company or force the management out? It was too much. And so, several of the dissenting shareholders joined our side. What's more, based on the work in the prior weeks of meeting with shareholders and those who couldn't attend, I'd collected a significant number of proxies. Those shareholders gave me their votes to use as I saw fit, and it was a difference maker. And when it came time to vote, I used those proxies to advance our corporate vision. The result was decisive. When the votes were tallied, an upset of sorts occurred, nixing one of my favorite board members. (We'd later reinstall him in a show of good faith.) And so, emerging from that meeting, we had alignment of vision and a clear mandate to continue the course.

Months after that contentious meeting, the board approved the strategy Anthony, Chris, and I had laid out. The company would offer to buy the shares of the group who wanted to force the sale, using the cash stores and an injection from a new investor. And that's exactly what we did.

With a fresh vote of confidence, we doubled down, put in everything we had. We invested more time, effort, and energy into the company we'd helped refound.

REFOUNDING CARE IN THE DELTA

Every Refounder I've met takes a sober look at the world around them, refocuses (kills their darlings), imagines better possibilities, and works to create better futures for others. What's more, each Refounder has the boldness to move on his convictions. One of the most striking examples of a Refounder is Dr. Foluso Fakorede, an interventional cardiologist in Bolivar County, Mississippi.

Born to Nigerian parents, Dr. Fakorede was raised in New Jersey. He pursued his dream of becoming a doctor, and after medical school, he took up a position as a vascular surgeon in Jackson, Tennessee. He was, by all accounts, a principled and forceful character, one who wanted the system to work as the system should. And when he became suspicious that his clinic was overcharging expenses, he reported those charges. As a result, he was terminated.

Out of a job and not knowing what was next, he decided to explore the medical needs of the people in the Mississippi Delta. He'd heard how the African American community of the region was underserved and wary of the medical-industrial complex. He'd heard that diabetic amputations were the norm in the region. What's more, Dr. Fakorede was moved by the disparity in health equity. Two maps illustrate this story well. One indicates the number of amputations due to peripheral artery disease in the United States, the other shows the concentration of the enslaved population in 1860. The concentrations of both populations were stunningly similar. Why?

As of 2016, the prevalence of diagnosed diabetes was highest among Native Americans (14.7 percent), Hispanics (12.5 percent), and African Americans (11.7 percent). By way of comparison, only 7.5 percent of the white population has been diagnosed with diabetes.[22] What's more, the concentration of diabetic patients is denser in the American South, a region often more rural, more racially segregated, and more economically depressed. So, it should come as no surprise that a larger concentration of chronic wounds and diabetic amputations occurs across the southern portion of the United States than anywhere else in the country, and therefore, that Black patients would be disproportionately affected.

As he considered the plight of Southern Black diabetics, as he considered how amputations increased the likelihood of death, Dr. Fakorede knew what he had to do. He headed south to scout the situation for himself. And after a visit to Cleveland, Mississippi, Dr. Fakorede's suspicions were confirmed. The experience of the African American diabetic in the Delta was nothing short of bleak.

He had other options on the table. He could have taken a well-paying job close to friends and family. He didn't, though. Without access to nutritious foods, relying on fatty, sugar-laden foods to get by, the people of Bolivar County, Mississippi, were more susceptible to diabetic amputation than diabetics in more affluent counties, and Fakorede knew it. Something had to change.

A *ProPublica* article published in 2020 described Dr. Fakorede's decision to move to the Delta this way:

> Fakorede had spent years studying health disparities: African Americans develop

---

22. "National Diabetes Statistics Report 2020," https://www.cdc.gov/diabetes/pdfs/data/statistics/national-diabetes-statistics-report.pdf.

chronic diseases a decade earlier than their white counterparts; they are twice as likely to die from diabetes; they live, on average, three years fewer. In the Delta, Fakorede could treat patients who looked like him; he could find only one other black interventional cardiologist in the entire state. A growing body of evidence had shown how racial biases throughout the medical system meant worse results for African Americans. And he knew the research—black patients were more responsive to, and more trustful of, black doctors. He decided after his trip that he'd start a temporary practice in Mississippi, and he rented an apartment deep in the Delta.[23]

After meeting with diabetic amputees and at-risk patients who were underserved and over-cut, he knew he could help. By opening up the patients' arteries, by increasing the blood flow to the areas of the wound with stents and balloons, Fakorede could bring new blood to areas of chronic wounding and could keep his patients from enduring amputations. And each amputation that was avoided was a potential life spared. It was a no-brainer. Fakorede sold his Tennessee home and opened a clinic in Cleveland, Mississippi.

He began to spread the word, going so far as to buy a billboard on the Delta's main thoroughfare, Highway 61, which

23. Lizzie Presser, "The Black American Amputation Epidemic," *ProPublica* (May 19, 2020), https://features.propublica.org/diabetes-amputations/black-american-amputation-epidemic/.

read, "Amputation Prevention Institute." He spread the word through the medical community, and with new credentials at Bolivar Medical Center, Fakorede began consulting on cases. The result? Since Dr. Fakorede's arrival, annual amputations due to vascular disease have dropped by over 75 percent.

As I spoke with Dr. Fakorede, it was clear his motivation is to right the wrongs of the health system, to take something broken and make something better. He reinvested in bringing equitable care to those who were often neglected. Sure, there's money to be made as a vascular surgeon. Sure, his standard of living and quality of life might be higher than those of his average patient. But if Dr. Fakorede wanted, I'm sure he could ply his trade in more lucrative ways. That's not what he has chosen to do. Instead, he has chosen to open his clinic in an economically depressed community with an underserved population. He has chosen to forgo the bright lights and big bucks in order to tend to the historically hurting. Why? I have to believe it's because he's driven by a bigger purpose. And the African American diabetic community in the Deep South is better off for it.

REFOUNDERS REINVEST IN BIGGER PURPOSES

If you've been in the trenches of a refounding process, particularly if you're fueled by a bigger purpose, you know just how rewarding it can be. With new success comes new opportunity, new ability to pour more resources into your bigger purpose. But so often, that success brings competing opinions.

Opinions of shareholders.

Opinions of the board of directors.

Opinions of your partner, wife/husband, or fellow community organizers.

When times are bad, everyone has an opinion. In the middle of this kind of opinion vortex, it can be easy to lose sight of what really matters—your bigger purpose.

Investing in bigger purposes is no small task. It requires unfettered belief and the discipline to follow through on that belief. That follow-through is what I call reinvesting in your bigger purpose. But how do Refounders do this?

1. TAKE A SOBER LOOK: REFOUNDERS LISTEN

Before deciding how to best reinvest in their bigger purpose, Refounders listen. They listen to their shareholders, their board of directors, and their fellow partners. They listen to their clients and customers, too. They don't listen to refute, but rather to suss out what course of action might serve the bigger purpose.

In those early days of growth and profitability, we listened to all opinions. We listened to the shareholders that agreed with us and those who dissented. We listened to those who thought we should change course, but we also listened to our guts. Together, Anthony, Chris, and I listened and made the most sober judgment we could. We wouldn't pursue ideas that competed with our bigger purpose. Instead, we'd double down. We'd reinvest in our company so that we could pursue our bigger purpose.

2. REFOUNDER'S FOCUS: REFOUNDERS LEAD CONSENSUS

When faced with numerous opinions, it's important to identify those who want to advance personal agendas and those who want to advance the bigger purpose of the company. And when you find those whose vision aligns with the bigger purpose of the organization, build coalitions and consensus with them.

A few of us were clear on our bigger purpose. What's more, we were clear on the kind of corporate culture we'd need to pursue and make strides toward that bigger purpose. We believed that if we chased that purpose, the profits would come, and in fact, we had proven that was true. And so, before that fateful proxy war with certain members of the board of directors, we identified those shareholders who were like-minded, who understood the direction we were heading. We listened to their ideas, and they listened to ours. Together, we forged a coalition of people who were so committed to the bigger purpose of Net Health that we decided to go all-in.

3. IMAGINING NEW POSSIBILITIES: REFOUNDERS REINVEST IN POSSIBILITIES, NOT CERTAINTIES

There are times when commitments to bigger purposes and coalition-building will be enough. But in every refounding situation—whether in your company, community of faith, or marriage—there will be times when you and the coalition of purpose-oriented partners have to take a radical step and take the plunge. You have to take a risk, reinvesting in possibilities, not certainties.

You might have to pool your resources and invest in the time, talent, or tools it takes to advance your bigger purpose. You might have to raise capital from like-minded investors or get a loan from a bank in order to take out opposition. You might have to sell your house or car and move to the Delta. If you're dealing with a failing community or marriage, you may have to adjust your schedule to invest more time in relationships. And the truth is, those kinds of reinvestment might be risky. They might not pan out. Still Refounders reinvest in their bigger purpose in order to recognize ultimate rewards.

This was the approach Dr. Fakorede took. It was the approach we took, too. We listened to both supporters and detractors and considered their feedback. From that group, we identified those who would join a coalition of people, and we partnered with them. Together, that coalition committed. We bought out the dissenters, those who disagreed with the bigger purpose and who threatened to derail our direction. And that risk ultimately paid off.

It bears noting that this will not be an easy process. There might be very good people who don't want to join in your risk-taking reinvestment. They might not be aligned with your bigger purpose, particularly in a profit-only, shareholder-first society. And if their purposes differ from yours, if you find yourself in terse conversations (or a brutal proxy war), this does not mean they are evil, shortsighted, or ignorant. It simply means they're not the coalition you need to pursue your bigger purpose.

4. CREATING BETTER REALITIES: BETTER REALITIES START WITH REINVESTING IN PEOPLE

With the proxy war in our rearview mirror and with a clear mandate to pursue the Net Health purpose, we doubled down on our efforts. We believed capitalism could change the culture at large, that it could advance human flourishing. But to do that, we knew we had to start in-house. After all, if we couldn't create a culture of human flourishing for our employees, what right would we have to preach the importance of culture change to the world around us?

So, we set out to build an internal coalition of employees who understood the bigger purpose, which was to bring healing and hope to patients suffering from chronic wounds by providing excellent software to the caregivers who serve them. We invested in the interview process, did our best to identify those who cared more about the patients than they did about the money. As we started adding employees, we invested in training classes to ensure our employees were on the same page. We made sure they understood their unique strengths, our story, and more importantly, our company purpose—to create and deliver software products that would bring hope and healing to the patients.

We invested in a new employee training class, and there, we emphasized being vulnerable in order to drive authenticity and develop strong risk-taking muscles. We stressed the importance of teamwork and collaboration. Once the employees were onboarded, we did our best to provide above-average benefits that would give them the feeling of safety and security—healthcare, 401(k) benefits, and salaries that were competitive.

As we grew, as we began to realize the benefits of investing in our culture in order to change culture, we got even more granular. I began gathering teams in informal settings to chat about work problems. I'd call a meeting and ask the group whether they'd like to spend an hour in a conference room or head out to the Strip District to talk over coffee or a French pastry at the new bakery. Sometimes, we'd stop to get coffee on the way if a new espresso joint popped up. Before any of those impromptu meetings, I'd start with a few corny icebreakers— *What was your favorite television show when you were thirteen?* or *What's your favorite album of the last ten years?* or *Beatles or Stones?*

We were growing, getting to know each other, and accomplishing big things. Why? Because we were committed to the same purpose. And together, we were investing in it. It was that collective investment that turned Net Health into what it is today. A thriving company that serves its clients? Yes, but that's only part of the story.

Years later, with a lot more growth, focus, and vigilance, the reinvestment in the company would pay off. A steady stream of private equity investors came knocking, and they presented us with a couple of options. We could sell the entire company and walk. Alternatively, they could invest in the company and connect us with specialized knowledge and expertise. We could become the platform for other healthcare software solutions.

Knowing we still had upside and that with an additional cash infusion we could make additional investments into underserved growth markets, we partnered with one of those private equity funds, and they invested heavily. They acquired a controlling stake, but they left the core team intact. Anthony joined as a full partner in the company and became the chairman/CEO. So, with new opportunities and new inflows, we doubled down again. We invested even more heavily in our people and our purpose. And looking back, I can see just how much it paid off.

REFOUNDER TAKEAWAYS

- Refounders reinvest their time, talent, and money in their bigger purpose.
- Refounders listen and lead by building consensus.
- Refounders always invest in people.

EIGHT

CREATE BETTER CULTURES

We'd gone from the brink of bankruptcy to being courted by some of the most notable investors in the world. Publications were taking notice. The likes of *Inc.* (the magazine), the Initiative for a Competitive Inner City, and *Modern Healthcare* featured our company in some way. We were named one of the best places to work by the *Pittsburgh Business Times.* I was even featured on the cover of *TEQ Magazine.* What's more, Chris and I were recognized with the Ernst & Young Entrepreneur of the Year award. But as exciting as all of that coverage was, it would have been meaningless to us if the culture had been a drag. And though it was pretty good, we believed it could be better.

With a fundamental belief that thriving companies could change the culture, we set out to imagine an even better working environment, a place where the people knew they fit in and had a huge part to play in the success of the company. We wanted to create an environment that felt more like a community and less like work. And when I thought about what that might look like, I imagined my experience at summer camp.

Summer camp?

In college, I had the privilege of working as a counselor at Sheldon Calvary Camp, bordering Lake Erie, which hosted students from elementary school to high school. Campers were mostly regional, but some came from around the United States, many were away from their parents for the first time. They were thrown into a cabin with a dozen other strangers. They were forced to forge fast friendships and learn to live with people different from them. And if you've ever been to summer camp as a kid, you might remember just how frightening and exciting it can be.

The counselors were tasked to create a culture where every camper felt safe, valued, and honored. And as a counselor, I didn't need a set of rules and regulations to know how to create that atmosphere, although there was a mostly oral history of how to do this well. I put myself in the shoes of the campers, asked what would make me feel included in this awkward camp experience. I also learned from the counselors and camp leaders who'd been there for years and saw how they went out of their way to include each camper. I watched how this spirit of inclusion and safety made the weeks so much better, and each session set us up for a grand finale.

At the conclusion of each session, we threw a party. We celebrated the campers, handed out achievement and spirit awards, and shared our favorite experiences. We pointed the children toward what was true and beautiful about each of them, and they followed suit, often sharing what their fellow campers had meant to them over the week. After the award ceremony, we feasted and danced late into the night. Everyone was included. Everyone was seen. And when the parents came to pick up their kids the following day, we listened as they shared how much fun they'd had, the new friends they'd made, and the awards they'd received.

We worked hard to create a winning culture at camp. The result? Most campers came back year after year. Some even went on to become counselors themselves, passing that same culture down to the next generation. The spirit of inclusion and celebration led to camper retention and fierce loyalty (as indicated by the fact that I'm talking about it more than two decades later). For many, this was a coming-of-age experience where they first tasted freedom (both counselors and campers), danced at bonfires, and were forced to engage others dissimilar from them and their daily routine.

Talking to friends and colleagues from around the country, I noted that a similar spirit of inclusion and celebration was sorely lacking in corporate America. If I was really honest, we had a lot of work to do. And though I didn't want to create lanyards and run ropes courses, I wondered: *How could we create a culture of safety, freedom, and celebration in the day-to-day life of our company?*

I shared my thoughts with the core team. Chris was on board. So was Anthony, which came as no surprise, because he'd been a huge proponent of creating meaningful culture when we were just a fledgling team. In fact, Anthony had seeded the idea of creating better cultures by example.

CREATING CULTURE IS A MARATHON

In the earliest days of refounding, Anthony—then chairman of the board—met with me on a weekly (and sometimes daily) basis. Waist-deep in a corporate-salvaging pivot, it was important to keep him abreast of new developments, new opportunities, and potential pitfalls. As president, that job fell to me. But our meetings weren't just for information sharing. Anthony was a seasoned businessman, and he provided sage advice about business, internal culture-making, and work-life balance. As I sought to steer the company in a more prosperous direction, I found myself leaning more and more on his advice.

Anthony wanted me to become the best version of myself, both professionally and personally. We scouted a start-up cafe led by an up-and-coming local chef named Rick DeShantz and chose his relatively unknown joint as the venue for hashing out a few work issues. Between bites of a prosciutto sandwich, Anthony called me out with a series of questions.

"Are you a runner?"

I laughed between bites. What kind of question is that over a large lunch? And surely he already knew the answer to the question just by looking at me. While I enjoyed some weight training, I wasn't the paragon of cardiovascular health.

"Seriously," he said, "are you a runner?"

I stalled, hemmed and hawed, told him I wanted to think about my answer. But I knew the answer. I'd played a little lacrosse in college, skateboarded in my younger years, and toyed with the romantic notion of rowing. But was I a runner? No. Did I want to be? Hardly.

Anthony was my polar opposite when it came to athletics.

He was a multi-time marathoner and had recently completed his third triathlon. He trained his body and mind to go the distance, and not wanting to disappoint him, even though it was wholly unrelated to work, I fibbed.

"Occasionally."

He offered no response.

"I mean, not really."

He offered a sort of knowing smile. That's when I knew he had me in a sort of trap.

"Ever thought of running a marathon?"

It was posed as a simple question, but it felt like a test. Could he see the sweat beads forming on my forehead? Did he sense my deep antipathy for running? He must have, because he let the question hang. And the longer it did, the more I knew where this conversation was heading.

I ran the calculus. If I said no, what would Anthony think? Would he think I wasn't willing to dig deep and try new things? Would he think I didn't have the internal drive to compete at the highest levels of business? After all, he'd had a meteoric rise through the healthcare industry, in no small part because of his iron will, mental toughness, and fierce competitive spirit. If I wasn't strong-willed enough to run a marathon, wouldn't that say something about me?

But what if I agreed? I'd have to endure the torture of long-distance running. Worse, what if I couldn't handle the training and bailed at the point where my pain overcame my will to impress a board member?

It was a classic Catch-22. What if I could just play it cool, pass it off as his attempt to share some business metaphor with me?

"I've never really considered it. What's it like?"

Anthony shared about the training and methodology, how it was all about expansive progress. And the same disciplines required to run a marathon were useful in running a business, he told me. Marathoners had to be mentally fit, up for a difficult task of endurance, and iron-willed enough to keep going when the desire to keep going was all but gone. He regaled me with war stories about endurance events, and as he did, I realized his play. He was testing my mettle as a future business partner. If I was going to ride with Anthony, I'd have to prove myself first.

"I'd like you to be my training partner for my next marathon," he said.

Had I heard that right? Not only did he want me to run an ungodly number of miles, but he wanted me to train with him, a man who, compared to me, was all but a professional endurance athlete? It was an insane thought, and I told him as much. But my incredulity didn't faze him. He'd help me ramp up, he said, and acting as a sort of mentor in the process would help him stay accountable for getting himself into marathon shape.

Anthony was offering me an opportunity. So, after discussing it that night with Jen, I mustered the conviction and said, "I'm in. What's involved?"

Anthony laid out a plan, and the next morning I laced up my shoes and started jogging. I built up slowly, running every morning for a month until I could plow through five miles at a strong pace. Most mornings, Jen ran with me. She is a natural runner, smiling and singing as she goes. And after I'd built up my endurance, we called Anthony and told him we'd both join him for the training.

We met at a local trail on a Saturday morning, and as he stepped out of his car in his running clothes, I was struck with this odd feeling that I had taken off my business face and exchanged it for my weekend self. I was still a little on edge, but spending time running together with Jen felt different than I thought business was supposed to feel. I told him I was still slow, apologizing for the fact that I was sure to hold him back. He didn't say much, just smiled and said, "Let's go."

Anthony and Jen were more agile, their paces quicker. But to my surprise—and relief—Anthony didn't force me to keep up. Instead, he adjusted the group pace to my own, and as he did, I began to trust that he wouldn't push me beyond my physical and psychological limits. When we finished that first run, I felt inspired, motivated, and accomplished.

Over the coming weeks, Anthony would continue to take the same approach. He'd lead me through hill workouts and speed workouts, sticking with me as I built up my base running fitness. On our longer runs, he only pushed the pace for short intervals. And during all these workouts, we were able to chat about organizational stuff.

What about licensing issues and our intellectual property?

What were the best strategies for selling and implementing?

How should we run board meetings?

Week after week, my cardio thresholds increased, as did my mental toughness. Even more, though, my trust and relationship with Anthony grew. There was nothing we couldn't talk about, and the longer we ran together, the more we grew comfortable *not* talking. Some mornings, we'd plow the hills of Sewickley Heights, enjoying the simple pleasure of a morning sunrise. We built from a base of miles to minutes, exchanging little numbers like six, seven, or eight miles for larger numbers like running for 100, 150, or 200 minutes as the goal.

The months passed quickly, and we were ready. Anthony had chosen an idyllic venue for the marathon—Big Sur, California. We'd start the race in a redwood forest, making our way out of the trees and onto Highway 1, where we'd run along the coast of paradise. It was an exclusive event—so exclusive, in fact, that we had to enter a lottery months earlier in order to secure our slots. And as we boarded the plane with our wives, a nervous energy crept up. There was no turning back.

Race day came, and with it, a new experience. I stood near the back of the mass of people waiting to run. They were triple-checking their liquids, their caffeine beans, the energy gels in their fuel belts. Long lines formed outside the port-a-johns, as the body's natural diuretic—adrenaline—kicked in. The man in front of me paced in tiny circles. The woman beside me stretched her quads for the twentieth time. The man to my right chatted to no one in particular. I supposed I wasn't alone in my first-marathon jitters.

The race began, and I looked up at the majestic redwoods. It was the application of discipline and incremental growth that brought me here. But it was also the goodwill and intention of Anthony that made me believe I could do something special. He'd been patient, created an atmosphere where I could succeed. And now, here I was, pounding an almost magical pavement and knowing I was up to the task.

Anthony and I ran every step together. I was careful to stick to my pace as I took in the wonder around me. As I exited the forest, the sight of the beach kept me inspired for the next forty-five minutes, all the way to the base of the much-hyped Hurricane Point. I made the 2.2-mile climb, inspired to push ahead by the breath-taking views. I crossed the Bixby Bridge, which was built in 1932 and showcases the beauty of Big Sur's rocky coastline. As I surveyed the coast, I realized I was grinning, even through the pain.

As I crossed the finish line, I was grateful I'd accepted Anthony's challenge. He'd believed in me, created a running culture in which I could thrive, and helped me navigate a difficult training regimen. Through it all, we'd built a strong relationship and a culture of cooperation because we were enduring something together. And throughout the entire process, I came to learn what Anthony already knew. The culture of any enterprise (whether corporate enterprise or the enterprise of completing a marathon) is a leading indicator of success.

REFOUNDING CULTURE

Culture is a buzzword these days. Every company wants to have "amazing corporate culture" or a "winning culture" or a "progressive, inclusive, collaborative culture." Often, companies go about it in all the wrong ways, thinking they can buy great culture. They shell out the cash for a break-room ping-pong table or invest in a few hammocks for the courtyard. They might run a Friday beer cart through the office or offer an inexhaustible supply of exotic, single-origin teas. Yoga mats, massages, dog days—these might be good things, but none of them will improve your culture in the long term without underlying plans in place to achieve a greater cultural shift.

How do you create healthier cultures, then? You invest

in programs, processes, and ways of being that create an atmosphere where people feel seen, celebrated, and encouraged to be the best version of themselves. You pay fairly. You demonstrate and celebrate empathy, commitment, teamwork, and authenticity. You encourage your people to do the hard things, assuring them you'll be with them along the way.

Brand building, profit making, product production—all of it flows from the culture. And I believe this to be true. Trendy websites and fancy logos might be wonderful. They may attract attention. But what happens when someone engages with your business, your non-profit, or your community leadership? Do they come away feeling tired and frustrated or energized and enthusiastic? When they experience what you value, they experience the real you. That experience—the way you answer the phone, the way you use language in your AI bot on your website, the way you implement your solution, your invoice—*that* represents your culture. And that culture says a lot more about your brand than your logo, website, or social media profiles.

So how do you build amazing cultures, places where participants radiate joy and enthusiasm? Looking back at my summer camp experience and my Big Sur marathon, I've reflected on what's required to create an amazing corporate culture, a culture where teammates feel honored and respected. Invest in the following five factors, you can create the kind of culture your employees, clients, and customers want.

1. TAKE A SOBER LOOK: HOW ARE YOU INVESTING YOUR TIME?

Like money, time is a resource. But when it comes to culture, investments of time often pay off more than monetary investments.

At Camp Calvary, we invested a week or two of time in our campers. We spent time with them, came to understand the things they cared about, tried to understand how we could better celebrate them. In the same way, Anthony took time out of his schedule and spent hundreds of hours training with me. He didn't need to train with me, but he knew investing time in me would have an impact beyond the redwood forest at Big Sur. The time we spent together would allow us to strategize about the business, but it would also increase my mental toughness. It would show me that I could do hard things. What's more, the time he spent with me assured me that I had a true teammate, someone who was in it with me for the long haul.

To create amazing culture, you have to allocate time. And by that, I do not mean spending a few minutes with a client or colleague for a quick one-on-one (though those are important). It doesn't mean simply sending a quick text to check in on someone every now and then (though that's important, too). If you intend to solve big problems, you have to invest quality time in your people. What's more, you have to teach them to invest quality time in the people around them. After all, if you're the leader of an organization, you might not have *enough* time to spend with every employee or member on a regular basis.

2. REFOUNDER'S FOCUS: CULTIVATING EMPATHY

Creating amazing culture requires empathy. Simply put, if you cannot understand and share in the feelings of those around you, you'll never create a culture worth having. I learned this in my earliest days at Camp Calvary. Without understanding our campers' fears and self-doubts, without understanding what motivated them, we couldn't give them the ultimate camp experience.

Anthony knew the importance of empathy, too. He remembered what it was like to be young and inexperienced, and as we ran he shared his own experiences, both his successes and his failures. He knew how terrifying the prospect of turning around a failing company must have been for an entrepreneur in his twenties. He met me where I was, listened to my concerns, and offered counsel. He met me where I was in my physical training, too. He matched my pace, never pushed me too far beyond my perceived limits. He coached me through the process, helped me push through the pain of the training. Through it, we connected on a deeper lever and formed a deep bond of trust. This trust building for risk-taking is true for all great relationships.

"Empathy fuels connection," writes popular author and sociologist Dr. Brené Brown.[24] And when I consider Dr. Brown's statement I see just how true that was for me. Anthony's show of empathy created space for me to be vulnerable. Vulnerability created space for an authentic give-and-take relationship. In that relationship, I felt the safety to take risks, even the risk of running a marathon. This is true in all enterprises. Ultimately it's the informed and engaged risk-taking that leads to growth.

---

24. Brené Brown, "Brené Brown on Empathy," YouTube.com (December 10, 2013), https://www.youtube.com/watch?v=1Evwgu369Jw (accessed November 21, 2020).

Over the years, we've worked hard to cultivate empathy and vulnerability in our corporate setting. As we have, we've watched as relationships have grown. With stronger relationships, we've seen teams take bigger risks, reap bigger rewards, and as a result, have bigger celebrations. Focusing on empathy has led to a culture worth celebrating.

3. IMAGINING NEW REALITIES: IMAGINE THE CULTURE YOU WANT TO CREATE

Anthony was able to imagine a new reality for me, a future I didn't even know I wanted. He knew inviting me into that imagined reality would strengthen our bond of trust if he acted in empathy and vulnerability. And he was right.

Where people cannot be themselves, when they cannot share their success, failures, and disagreements without fear of reprisal, you'll never have good corporate culture. If you're in that kind of environment, you have to imagine a better way of being. You have to imagine the sort of environment where others lean into empathy and vulnerability, where they can take risks, where they can share their opinions without fear of reprisal. And as we'll see in the next chapter, you even have to be able to imagine the sort of place where coworkers and teammates can challenge leadership without fear.

As we've seen throughout this book, imagination is critical to the refounding process. This is no less true than in the area of refounding a corporate culture. Without imagining the kind of culture you want to have, you'll never achieve it.

CREATING BETTER REALITIES: LOG THE MILES

You cannot roll off of the couch and run a marathon. You have to build cardiovascular stamina and muscle strength. You have to log the miles. If you're not committed to the practice, you'll never follow through. In the same way, you can't wake up one day and magically create amazing corporate culture. Culture creation requires a commitment to invest in your people. It requires a commitment to taking the time, to investing in empathy. It requires a commitment to living from your bigger purpose, to putting people over profits.

Chris and I set out to brainstorm a way to do this at scale. Together, we asked how we might create a more authentic, more empathetic, more team-oriented environment. We looked at how much time and money we could budget toward solving our cultural conundrum. We considered a dozen or more ideas, and as we discussed them, one emerged as the clear winner: Strategy Cafe.

We logged the miles, so to speak. We prepared for a company-wide gathering and set the budget. We set the itinerary, and the bulk of it consisted of investing time in solving the company's biggest problems. We troubleshot every conceivable roadblock. And when the day of the event came, we were prepared.

With the employees divided into small groups (an investment in teamwork), we identified issues facing our company, our clients, and those who were suffering from chronic wounds. The teams were tasked with thinking through those problems and brainstorming even the craziest solutions (an investment in authenticity). No ideas were off limits, none were too crazy, and everyone's contribution was due equal consideration (an investment in empathy). We wanted them to use every ounce of creativity and to build off one another. And we were committed to see it through.

As the inaugural Strategy Cafe drew to a close, we reviewed the solutions generated by the team. There were software solutions, client management solutions, and solutions to address internal cultural issues. Sure, there were some crazy ideas, but for the most part, the solutions were incredible. Some we implemented immediately. But as productive as the solutions were, the day spent on Strategy Cafe had an unintended consequence. We noticed a new sort of lightness in the office. There was more joy, more buy-in. This larger investment in building corporate culture created a new kind of energy. Our people were more connected, too. So, Strategy Cafe became a mainstay, and in the coming years we would expand it to an event we call Connect.

Our initial crack at cultural investment had paid off. It wasn't enough, though. We wanted to push harder, create better systems so that we could get the best out of our people. And that's exactly what we set out to do. We set out to listen, respond, and act in ways that bolster culture. Why? We believed that if we did, we'd foster a more creative, more collaborative environment that would produce better results. What's more, we believed we could impact more than just the culture at Net Health. We believed we could impact the culture at large.

REFOUNDER TAKEAWAYS

- Refounders invest in programs, processes, and policies that help people feel seen, celebrated, and encouraged.
- Refounders take a sober look, asking whether they are investing their time in building better cultures.
- Refounders believe that building a better culture produces better results, both for the company and in the world at large.

NINE

THE REFOUNDER'S MENTALITY

"How would you feel about bringing on a fellow?" Anthony asked yet another inciting question while we were feasting on Cuban sandwiches at Kaya in the Strip.

"What, like an intern?" I asked.

"Something like that," he said.

In between bites of sweet potato fries, he went on to share his own experience. After graduating from Duke, he'd taken a fellowship at Presbyterian Hospital, and it had given him real-world experience. He'd experienced firsthand what it was like to join the daily grind of corporate America. It was good, he said, but he wondered whether our community could offer something better than simple corporate experience. He wondered whether we might spread the good news of corporate culture to an up-and-comer. After all, if we really were intent on using the culture to influence the world, shouldn't we consider inviting some young people in to experience it?

It was a good idea, I admitted. Still, as someone who'd brought the company back from life-support and into the land of the living, I was cautious. I'd programmed myself to think through costs at the outset of any new hire and to examine whether that cost would have a direct impact on the company's financial health. And could a fellow really add value to our business?

Even more concerning, with about fifty employees, would the addition of a fellow have a negative impact on the office vibe? After all, adding a bummer of a teammate to a small team might be a real drag. I'd personally experienced this in business, not-for-profit work, and friendship groups.

Anthony must have noted my skepticism, because he pressed the issue. "There's a fellowship program in town," he said, "and they match recent college graduates with employers. If we take one on, they'll do their part to make sure it's the right person. You'll have direct impact in the process. And," he intoned with emphasis, "you'll get to mentor the person when they join the team."

And the difference between this and babysitting is? I wondered, but did not say it aloud.

The truth was, the prospect of mentoring a young college graduate was terrifying. I wasn't sure I had the time, and up to that point, I'd mostly worked with people at least ten years my senior. Could I be trusted with the leadership development of a young mind?

Anthony persisted. "Aren't there some jobs at the company where we could use an extra pair of hands?"

I sighed. He was right. We'd continued our growth trend of over 50 percent year-over-year for almost a decade. There was always more work to do than there were people to do it. And if we could get a young and ambitious fellow to tackle some of those projects, it might create margin for the rest of the team. And so, I agreed. Anthony would reach out to his contact, and I'd gather the team to outline the new fellowship program.

Over the weeks that followed, Chris and I met with Dana, our director of life (our creative title for our human resources director). Together, we imagined a program that would give our new fellow exposure to the whole company, one that rotated them through the various departments. Each week, the program would require four days of work and a half-day of training. We'd make sure the chosen fellow had plenty of time to explore the city, to get to know the shops and people in the Strip District. After all, we often drew comparisons between the refounding of our company and the refounding of the Strip District.

We finalized our program and contacted the fellowship coordinators. Weeks later, we were matched up with our new fellow, Billy.

He was quiet and intense, and that was evident from his first handshake. He didn't exhibit the normal bluster of most young, energetic business people (including me when I was his age). He moved with purpose, with intention, and was kind to everyone he met. As we walked him through the departments, he asked the best questions. Day one, and already we knew Billy was a fit.

Over the following months, Chris, Anthony, and I took turns taking Billy to lunch. He joined an in-house soccer team with Chris. He took me up on coffee break and happy hour offers. He quickly made fans and gained quite the following because of his ability to listen and contribute to solutions. He was often the first to volunteer for a mundane task, leading by example in every way. He was quick with a smile, and though his humor was dry, it was razor-sharp. We couldn't have found a better fit.

As I got to know Billy better, I began to see that his intensity was not put on. It was sincere, and if he didn't understand a particular part of the business, he devoted himself to learning. He was bent on contributing, on growing as a leader. And, after nine months of hosting Billy as a fellow, we brought him on full-time. He was sincere, earnest, hardworking, and, we felt, the embodiment of our ethos through and through.

More than a year later, Billy was knocking it out of the park. And just when we thought he was completely bought in and an exemplar of our culture, things took a turn. One morning, I woke to an email Billy had sent our entire leadership team at 1:00 a.m., and because nothing good happens after midnight (that's what my mother used to say), I braced for the worst.

Was Billy rage emailing?

Was he drunk emailing?

Worse yet, was he resigning?

In the opening paragraphs, he noted some organizational problems, areas where we might be underperforming or perhaps not performing at all. He noted the common problem in each of those areas. Simply put, we were focusing on a few of the wrong things. He took it a step further and volunteered to buy each of us a book on a management practice he thought would help.

Did I read that right? A kid fresh out of college with virtually no savings, living on a starter salary, had offered to buy a half-dozen books for the leadership team?

I re-read the sentence, and sure enough, he'd offered to buy us a book. There was a catch, though. He'd only make the investment if we committed to reading the first chapter. AS A TEAM.

I finished the email and sat at my desk, astounded. These were not the ramblings of an inebriated, disgruntled employee. The entire email was so cogent, so articulate, and so well thought out, that I couldn't help but respect this brass. After all, how many young employees would send that kind of an email to the higher-ups, especially higher-ups like Anthony, whose résumé was impeccable. Still, my cheeks burned.

I read the email again, looking for holes in his logic. And it was on that second reading that I realized I was allowing my ego to get in the way of some very valid criticism. The truth was, I'd never known Billy to be combative, brash, or cynical, so if he was willing to take this kind of risk, maybe it was worth my attention. Besides, we were always preaching vulnerability and authenticity to the team, and hadn't he taken a massive vulnerability risk? Wasn't he sharing feedback as authentically as he knew how? If I didn't give Billy's email a fair reading, I wasn't living by our cultural values.

It was time to listen. So, the leadership team carved out some time and considered his email together. We examined Billy's premise. After spending a year with us, he had noticed a gap. We had larger goals, but we often struggled to chart a clear path to reach those goals because of the speed of the organization. And without a clear path, how could we measure our progress from waypoint to waypoint?

We had targets, of course, but Billy's foundational premise was that those targets were aspirational, and over time, we couldn't keep hitting aspirational targets accidentally. He cited our most prominent goal: double in size within the next fifteen months. It sounded like a great rallying cry or talking point at the year-end meeting. It even looked good in our board books. But what were the incremental steps to achieving this goal, and could we explain them to every team member? How were we measuring behaviors to see whether we were on track?

Our biggest problem, and the problem Billy had keenly recognized, was that we had fallen prey to common business *faux pas*. We were using a long list of *lagging* indicators as measures of our success instead of minding the *leading* indicators. Our goals had become the end results, and we weren't managing the smaller steps it would take to get us to where we wanted to be. It was an opportunity area, and we all realized it.

Billy bought us that book—*The 4 Disciplines of Execution: Achieving Your Wildly Important Goals*[25]—and it described this difference between leading and lagging indicators in detail. A *lagging indicator* is the measurement you want to achieve in the future—having a product line hit $100 million in revenue, for example. But when you focus solely on the lagging indicator, you bypass the *leading indicators*, the things that predict whether you will achieve your desired outcome, things like landing new client presentations, investing in research and development, and researching new technology, for instance. And if you

---

25. Chris McChesney, Sean Covey, and Jim Huling, *The 4 Disciplines of Execution: Achieving Your Wildly Important Goals* (New York: Free Press, 2012).

don't identify and measure your leading indicators, you won't consistently reach your lagging indicator goals.

Need it put in more practical terms?

Consider a simpler example. You might want to lose ten pounds. Will a daily weight check in help? Hardly. Instead, it only provides a measurement of a lagging indicator. But measuring how you eat, how many days you work out, how you sleep—all leading indicators—will help you predict whether you'll reach your weight loss goal. So, if you want to lose ten pounds, don't use your daily weigh-in—a lagging indicator— as the only measurement of progress. Focus instead on leading indicators, the most important things that contribute to the results you want. Institute a meal plan. Do a high-intensity interval training workout every day. Track whether you're eating after 7:00 p.m. Fast once a week. Then, measure how you're doing in each category. If you hit those leading indicators with consistency, there's a fair chance you'll reach your goal.

Sounds obvious, doesn't it? The sad truth is, though, given the pace of the growth, it wasn't super obvious to us until Billy raised the issue. In a very real sense, we were trying to hit an aggressive weight goal (albeit a weight-gain goal) without more precisely measuring the activities that might get us there. It was a leadership oversight, a form of corporate groupthink that needed refounding, and Billy identified it. And as a Refounder in his own right, he'd done the unthinkable; he'd confronted the leadership team. Why? Because that's what Refounders do.

Refounders are always trying to take broken systems and make them better. They know that seasons of growth and prosperity can obscure cracks. What's more, they know that in times of stress, those cracks become full-on fissures. And so, developing a Refounder's mentality requires active examination, a constant commitment to asking *What is?* and turning to *What ought to be?* And Refounders aren't content to ask those questions only of themselves. Refounders encourage others to participate in those questions.

A REFOUNDER IN A VUCA(R) WORLD

Over the course of my career, I've met many who have developed a Refounder's mentality and who work tirelessly to train others to think similarly. Among them is Dr. Chris Howard, president of Robert Morris University, a professionally focused, nationally ranked, doctoral-granting university in Pittsburgh named after a signer of the Declaration of Independence.

Dr. Howard didn't arrive at his current position in the traditional way. Instead of rising through the ranks of the academic world, Dr. Howard parachuted in. What do I mean?

Dr. Howard attended the United States Air Force Academy, where he played football and ultimately received a degree in political science. For his hard work in the classroom, he was awarded the Campbell Trophy, the highest academic award in the country presented to a senior college football player. A Rhodes Scholar, he went on to attend the University of Oxford, where he received a doctorate in politics. He didn't stop there. Continuing on to Harvard Business School, Dr. Howard earned his master's in business administration.

His academic career was rich. His military career was just as impressive. He served as a helicopter pilot in the Air Force Reserves and went on to become an intelligence officer for the elite Joint Special Operations Command. Returning to active duty during 2003, just as he was graduating from Harvard Business School, he was deployed to Afghanistan, where he served with distinction. His service was so distinctive, in fact, that he earned the coveted Bronze Star, a decoration awarded for heroic achievement or meritorious service in a combat zone.

At the conclusion of his military service, Dr. Howard enjoyed a successful career in the business world, serving at both General Electric and Bristol-Myers Squibb. And though he could have continued climbing the corporate ladder, he took a different path. He wanted to bring what he'd learned in his varied career to the educational system, a system he believed was in need of fresh thinking. Put another way, he could use what he'd learned to engage in a little educational refounding.

In the years preceding his presidency at RMU, he held the office of president at Hampden-Sydney College, the tenth oldest college in the United States, which was founded near Richmond, Virginia in 1775. While there, he saw what others could not. Major stress cracks existed in academia. The traditional classroom setting in which one teacher lectured twenty students seemed unsustainable, particularly with the rising cost of tuition. Students were unwilling to pay for college, especially if it meant relocating for a four-year experience, and increasingly, they were unwilling to take on the debt. What's more, with the advent of disruptive educational technology, much of the university infrastructure was threatened. After all, if you could host an online lecture, did you need a building full of lecture halls?

Speaking at the Black Student Forum at the Darden

School of Business at UVA, Dr. Howard didn't hold back. The university system was ripe for disruption, he said, noting, "The key challenges facing educators and educational institutions have to do with resources and innovation."[26] The traditional educational model of the classroom was being challenged, he said, and higher education needed to innovate or die.

It was a talk delivered almost nine years ago, and as it turns out, it was prophetic, particularly as COVID-19 swept the globe and changed the educational landscape. And though no one in higher education could have seen COVID coming, Dr. Howard's comments show that he understood something critical about the world in general and the world of higher education specifically. He understood that every system is prone to disruption, especially when no one is minding the cracks.

I've known Dr. Howard for several years and we've been engaged on several creative projects in and around the city. I've also spoken to the students at RMU, which led me to talk through his approach to leadership, particularly in light of so much chaos. And as we spoke, he shared that true leaders examine their organization in light of the VUCA(R) world in which we live.

Huh?

VUCA, he says, is an acronym that comes from the leadership theories of Warren Bennis and Burn Nanus, first used in 1987. According to Bennis and Nanus, the world is Volatile, Uncertain, Complex, and Ambiguous.[27] Dr. Howard adds the

---

26. "Dr. Christopher Howard on Challenges," YouTube.com (December 19, 2011), https://www.youtube.com/watch?v=OXCi25fqiBo.

27. https://www.vuca-world.org/

R at the end of the acronym, signifying that we live in a world that's VUCA in "Real Time." But what does this mean?

V—VOLATILE

Consider our COVID world for example. As the virus spread, everything became more volatile. The supply of toilet paper and cleaning products disappeared almost overnight. Demand for coffee-shop lattés dried up as people were forced to stay in their homes. Volatility in most sectors was off the charts, and the stock market swung wildly. Education shifted to online platforms, almost overnight in some places. Volatility, it seemed, was here to stay. And this volatility disrupted those who were not prepared for it.

U—UNCERTAIN

What was the world, if not uncertain, in the wake of the pandemic? The ways things had played out in the past—particularly in Dr. Howard's field of education—had very little to do with how they would play out in the future. Because of the volatility, because you couldn't know how state and local governments would handle the outbreak, future planning became all but impossible. Every plan required a backup plan, and every backup plan required a set of contingencies. In fact, as I spent time with Dr. Howard in preparation for this book, there remained uncertainty about RMU's upcoming academic year. And that uncertainty was not relegated to RMU. This kind of uncertainty was injected into every educational system across the country.

C—COMPLEX

COVID represented the introduction of a new complexity into an already complex world. It was as if a grain of sand had been introduced into a precision machine. And this new complexity created further stress on our already complex economic, educational, and political systems. What's more, we were forced to come up with complex solutions to these complex problems. At many schools across the country, for instance, new online learning modules were developed on the fly. In some cases— including at RMU—students could choose to attend socially distanced in-person classes, pre-recorded classes, online live classes, or some combination of these. What had already been complex was made more complex by many degrees.

A—AMBIGUOUS

In an environment of constant information streams, constant data, and conflicting opinions, it can be difficult to make sense of the world. In the era of COVID, for instance, information seemed to change daily. Doctors disagreed on which therapeutics worked and which didn't. Researchers seemed to disagree about whether masks prevented the spread of the disease. For every data point supporting quarantine, there was another data point (even if dubious) supporting attempts to achieve herd immunity by continuing business as usual. All of this led to a certain sort of ambiguity, an inability to make meaning from the messages being received. This kind of ambiguity disrupted decision-making for business owners, faith leaders, and educators.

(R)—REAL TIME

Dr. Howard adds an (R) to the VUCA framework, claiming that all of these elements—volatility, uncertainty, complexity, and ambiguity—operate in real time. And so, as he was planning for the 2020–2021 school year, he was forced to make adjustments on the fly. He drew on all his training—military strategic planning, business training, and academic expertise—to refound an educational system that could function in a VUCA(R) world.

This world isn't getting any less VUCA(R). And as Dr. Howard notes, careers aren't either. In the modern age, careers are filled with volatility, uncertainty, complexity, and ambiguity, and changes happen in real time. Industry disruption—whether from technology, innovation, or pandemic intervention—is a reality of the modern world. And when industry disruption happens, career-path disruption often comes with it. This is why the corporate ladder of yesterday has all but disappeared, Dr. Howard says. Instead of graduating from college, joining the workforce, and climbing the corporate ladder to the top, the modern workforce swings along what he calls "corporate monkey bars," often shifting from one career path to the next. And as they go, they use the momentum of their experience to carry them from one bar to the next.

This can be a good thing for those who are prepared, Dr. Howard notes. After all, the skills you learn at your initial corporate job might be just the things that set you up to be a successful freelancer. The skills you learn as a successful free-lancer might allow you to step into a more prominent corporate role. And this isn't just Dr. Howard's hunch. Instead, it's backed by his own life experience. It's backed by the data, too.

In fact, most millennials and members of Gen-Z will change jobs five to seven times. But they're not necessarily changing jobs because they want to—they are changing jobs because of rapid disruption, whether from innovation, technology, or other more chaotic forces.

Dr. Howard aims to prepare his students for the realities of the VUCA(R) world. He's demonstrating how a diverse background opens doors in a world in flux. He's teaching them to prepare for disruption, to look for it, and to address it using the sum of their education and experiences.

Dr. Howard and his team have created an educational model that's prepared for whatever the pandemic VUCA(R) world throws at them, whether through in-person classes, hybrid learning, or online-only classes. And in this way, Dr. Howard (and so many other educators around the country) are functioning as real-time Refounders. They are using their collective experience to see the gaps in the educational system and address them in real time.

CULTIVATING A REFOUNDER'S MENTALITY

Billy and Dr. Howard are both Refounders. And though the connection between them may not be evident at first blush, consider what they share in common—a Refounder's mentality. What are the characteristics of a Refounder's mentality?

1. TAKE A SOBER LOOK: REFOUNDERS IDENTIFY AND ANTICIPATE CHALLENGES

As we've seen throughout this book, Refounders are not content with the way things are. They identify Problem Zero, the problem that will inhibit future growth. As Rebels of Ought, they look at the world around them—their businesses, communities, and even marriages—and ask *What ought to be?* Even more, they anticipate the challenges that might block those future potentials. They understand that the world is increasingly VUCA(R), and they consider potential sources of challenge.

By taking a sober look, Billy anticipated challenges to Net Health's continued growth trajectory if we did not learn to set and measure interim goals. In the same way, Dr. Howard anticipated challenges to the educational system based on the fact that we're living in an increasingly disruptive pandemic environment. This commitment to anticipating challenges gave each clarity of vision for the future.

2. REFOUNDER'S FOCUS: FOCUSING ON WHAT REALLY MATTERS

Billy understood that it was not enough to look at the lagging indicator, the end goal. Instead, we needed to focus on leading indicators, the indicators that would be predictive of our success. We had to measure new sales calls, support publication in scientific journals, and facilitate sprints for product innovation, all of which would inevitably lead to growth.

Likewise, Dr. Howard doesn't simply measure enrollment numbers. He's taken a hard look at the world around him and has asked whether the university has proper systems to deliver education to students in an ever-changing environment. If those systems are in place, after all, they'll have a direct impact on the enrollment at RMU and the success of its students.

To cultivate a Refounder's mentality, you'll need to ask what measurements might be predictive of future goals, and then focus on those leading indicators. Though Chris and I wouldn't have been able to put words to it at the time, this was actually the approach we took in the earliest days. We got granular, examined the expenses we needed to reduce and the products that needed investment. But as we grew, as things got more complex, we lost sight of that well-ordered focus. Ultimately, we owe a great debt to Billy for pointing that out.

3. IMAGINING NEW POSSIBILITIES: REFOUNDERS DON'T TAKE THE STATUS QUO

Refounder's don't make changes for the sake of making changes. That said, as they anticipate challenges on the horizon, they're unafraid to rethink everything. They imagine their place in the coming reality and highlight the problems that keep them from getting there, just like Billy did at Net Health and Dr. Howard did years before COVID struck. They'll challenge conventional wisdom or industry norms and take risks when needed in order to advance the bigger purpose.

4. CREATING BETTER REALITIES: REFOUNDERS AIM TO BUILD BETTER WORLDS

Neither Billy nor Dr. Howard are content to leave the world as they found it. No matter where they go or what they do, they aim to improve things. And examining the other characters we've explored in this book—John Wallace, Astro Teller, Dr. Foluso Fakorede, and Paula Faris, an upcoming example in chapter 10—we see how they exhibit this same core desire to build better communities, create more interesting companies, advance better ideas, and inspire better ways of life.

Our world is more chaotic than ever, perhaps more VUCA(R) than even Dr. Howard anticipated. But if we're to make it through this VUCA(R) world, only those who've cultivated a Refounder's mentality will be poised to make a difference. Only they can contribute to the solutions we so desperately need. So, take a note from Billy and Dr. Howard. Adopt a Refounder's mentality, and start asking: What will it take to build something that lasts, even into the uncertain future?

REFOUNDER TAKEAWAYS

- Refounders mind the gaps by asking what systems are broken, examining where improvements can be made, and anticipating future challenges that might affect any given system.
- Refounders focus on leading indicators instead of lagging indicators, knowing that measuring the proper leading indicators will help them achieve their goals.
- Refounders understand facing the challenges of a VUCA(R) world will require new, imaginative ways of thinking.

TEN

REAPING THE REWARDS

The music is pumping, and the baristas work double time to keep up with the demand of the morning coffee rush in the lobby of the August Wilson Center for African American Culture. The sprawling architectural gem is named after the two-time Pulitzer Prize–winning African-American playwright raised in the Hill District, who wrote a cycle of ten plays addressing the issues impacting the Black community throughout the twentieth century. This place is a hub of culture in Pittsburgh, and its theater holds over 1,000 people, perfect for the company-wide event we call Connect, the event that started as Strategy Cue.

A house band plays through their soundcheck as they prepare for the first gig of the day. I know that voice. It's Josh, the founder of a Pittsburgh band. Their music is tight, well-rehearsed.

I walk through the electric atmosphere that has taken hold

of the lobby, offering a few quick words to Erika, a friend and coworker who's flown in from Nashville. We look around, note the people who've arrived from all over the country. They've come for a day of celebration, a day to reconnect with coworkers, and they greet each other with the same phrase, "Happy Connect!" a greeting that's taken hold over the years.

"It's really amazing, right?" she says. I agree. This is just the kind of atmosphere we had imagined years earlier.

Folks were eating, drinking their coffee.

A group was dancing a little to the band's soundcheck.

Several hundred people take turns creating a living mural by taking colorful wire and cascading it through a range of their views illustrated on a giant board. Together their collective ideas are creating a giant work of art.

I tell Erika it's good to see her, but it's time to start the morning, and with that, I turn and make my way to the auditorium where my colleagues are mic'ing up. A few minutes later, I stand on the corner of the stage just as the lights flicker in the theater. It's go time. The crowd—all our employees—are funneling in, filling every seat on the floor level while the band, led by our general counsel and bona fide, multi-album artist rocks an original tune. When everyone settles in, I enthusiastically take the stage, welcoming the people to Connect.

It's a day of celebration, a day to party, I say, and the food, gifts, and entertainment are on us. I invite them to settle, tell them to get ready for an amazing group of speakers. And with that, I hand the stage over to the people who matter most. The employees.

Mimi Einstein bounces onto the stage to a 1980s R&B jam. She's wearing black from head to toe, prepped for the vibe. She's been with the company for years and needs no introduction. Still, how many people know one of her most personal stories, the story of the Tel Aviv bombing?

"There are three things you need to know about me," she says. "First, I'm spunky. Second, I love shoes. Third, I always follow my gut. Two of these three things saved my life."

It's a killer opening.

Mimi, a Jewish girl raised in America, left the States to study in Israel for six months. She attended Hebrew University for a few weeks, then joined a kibbutz—a collective farming community—in southern Israel. She describes it in almost romantic terms—the class experience, the work, the food, the partying. And after returning home for only five months, a longing set in. She had to get back to Israel.

With the blessing of her parents, she enrolled in Tel Aviv University. In her downtime, she taught English as a second language. Her evenings were spent shopping in the malls and street markets and eating in outdoor cafes. There were beaches and nightclubs, and as she shares photos, a portrait of paradise sets in. But if Tel Aviv is paradise, it's a dicey one.

On a Friday afternoon, Mimi made her way home from work. She was riding the bus, one of the last before the lines closed for Shabbat. As the bus pulled to a corner, she looked out the window, and through the open storefront of a shoe store, saw a pair of brown platform shoes she had to have. So, she did what any shoe-maven with cash to spend would do. She ran to the front of the bus, hounded the driver to stop and let her out. The driver reluctantly capitulated, and as she stepped onto the corner, as she entered the store, she had no idea how life-altering that decision would be.

While she was in the store waiting for a clerk, a massive explosion shook the streets of Tel Aviv. Windows rattled. Everything vibrated. The store patrons ran for the exits. Mimi rushed into the street with the mass of people from the surrounding buildings, and she turned in the direction of the bus she'd been riding moments before. There, a plume of black smoke reached up into the afternoon sky.

Mimi pauses, seems to choke up. The crowd sits on edge, holding their breath. Someone in the crowd claps as if to encourage her to continue. Then, the entire auditorium begins to clap. "Go on, you can do it!" someone yells from the back.

It was the early 1990s in Israel, she says, and the constant threat of war hung in the air. On that day, the threat became a reality. The bus Mimi had been riding just moments before had been the target of a terrorist attack. The bus driver who had graciously stopped the bus so she could follow her gut was dead, along with all those afternoon commuters. Mimi had been saved by her love of shoes, by following her gut.

I look across the auditorium. Some lean forward. Many cover their mouths in shock. Mimi is alive and a contributing member of our team because of a fashion choice. I cannot help but consider just how fragile life is. I wonder whether the crowd is, too.

She smiles as she shares about the preciousness of life and the lessons she has carried with her since that day in Tel Aviv. "Live like there's no tomorrow," she says, and her message strikes a chord. Finished, the crowd stands to applaud. For the story? Yes. Even more, though, I think the applause is motivated by a deep sense of gratitude. Mimi, our beloved coworker, could have been another casualty of violence.

Instead, she's here. Living. Breathing. In the flesh. And she's brought us face-to-face with our mortality, and in that, what matters most—each other. And though I can't prove it, my gut says we've all grown just a little bit closer.

If Mimi's story had been the only one, it would have been enough. But the stories keep coming. Maureen Bowen shares a story of personal health. After years of traveling and living a sedentary lifestyle, she decided she needed to take control of her health. And while shopping for clothes to take up a running habit, the sales person helping her commented on her "fluffy body," said she was a "fluffy chested woman." She could have taken offense, but instead, she used the shame as fuel.

Maureen began pounding the pavement, built up her endurance until she was half-marathon ready. And after completing that marathon, she decided to keep rolling. She combined running with her passion for travel, and before it was all over, she'd run half-marathons in 50 states. But then, everything in her world shifted. Diagnosed with cancer, the mental toughness she'd developed as a marathon runner paid off. She pressed through the treatments, and when she made it to the other side, she got back out on the road and finished her second 50-state half-marathon tour in 2018. What's more, she went on to finish full marathons in 30 states and four ultra-marathons—a race that is typically longer than 31 miles—all while enjoying the benefits of losing 100 pounds.

There are others, too. Amy Nichols, a wellness specialist in the human resources department, takes the stage and declares herself a proud introvert operating in an extroverted world. She shares how each of us were created to fit a unique role in society and how we cannot change who we're meant to be. So, she says, extroverts might see the introverts in their lives as inviting them to a quieter, more contemplative life. Introverts might learn how to be more assertive in the world from their more extroverted coworkers and friends. Either way, she says, we should all do our best to learn from each other, to celebrate the ways in which we are different.

The highlight—at least for me—comes when our normally straightforward chief financial officer, Patrick, drags a trunk onto the stage while wearing a red wig. He opens the truck, pulls props from it, and while doing his best Carrot Top impersonation shares about the company's financial health. What would otherwise be a dry presentation is nothing short of a completely entertaining and transparent view of our financials. It's a picture of how we can re-imagine a corporate social norm.

The day of celebration continues, and though many companies might take a company-wide meeting to focus only on the year's numbers, this is not our primary focus. Patrick's performance aside, we spotlight the stories that matter most— the stories of our people, our clients, and the problems we care about solving. As we listen, we come to know each other in much deeper ways.

When we began the refounding, we were focused on corporate survival. Over the years, though, we focused on creating something bigger, something more meaningful. Though we could have played it like so many other companies, though we could have focused solely on the numbers, we didn't. We carved out time to hear from our employees, even though it cost us productivity. We took the time to celebrate them, even though the expense was no small thing. We broke with conventional corporate wisdom, and as I listen to the amazing stories, a sense of satisfaction sets in. A small group of rebel Refounders had changed the course of the company. Now, a theater full of people was reaping the rewards. Today we are the Rebels of Ought.

REAPING THE REWARDS IS NOT JUST FOR CORPORATE REFOUNDERS

As I've argued, founders and Refounders share the same gene, expressed in different ways. Founders start with nothing and create something. Refounders take existing, often depleted assets, and alchemically transform them into rewarding opportunities. Refounders take something broken and make something better. They might transform an existing company, positioning it to thrive amidst new technological realities. They might renovate a neighborhood like John Wallace did, creating beauty from what was once rundown. They might remake an educational system that will withstand the challenges of a VUCA(R) world, just as Dr. Howard is. But Refounders might also refound in more personal ways.

Consider Paula Faris.

Paula did not come to broadcast journalism the usual way. She'd been innately curious as a child, asking so many questions her family nicknamed her "Paula 20 Questions." But despite being talkative and outgoing around her family, despite showing an aptitude for grilling her aunts, uncles, and parents' friends, things were different at school.

The daughter of a Lebanese immigrant and an Irish

Catholic mother, Paula was gifted with darker skin, a slight frame, and what she calls "unusually large" green eyes. As a result, she was the target of merciless teasing by her elementary peers. In her book, *Called Out: Why I Traded Two Dream Jobs for a Life of True Calling*, Paula writes,

> They teased me as I walked down the hall, called me "Paula fish eyes" or "guppy." In the lunchroom, they spoofed the song Ernie used to sing on *Sesame Street*, taunting— "Guppy, guppy, you're the one; you make bath time lots of fun...." On more occasions than not, I walked to my mom's car at the end of the day, head down, dragging. Sometimes there were tears.[28]

What began as childhood teasing took root in Paula's life and grew into full-on self-doubt. She attended Cedarville University, and because she was inclined to the endless questioning of investigative reporting, she majored in broadcast journalism. She excelled in the program, and her professors knew she could have a promising career in the newsroom. Still plagued with fear and doubt, Paula refused to step in front of the camera. And so, after graduation, she didn't follow her gifts (what she'd later adopt as her "vocational calling"). Instead, she took an easier road and accepted a job selling radio spots for a local ad agency.

It was easy work, and she performed well. But then, like so

---

28. Paula Faris, *Called Out: Why I Traded Two Dream Jobs for a Life of True Calling* (Bloomington, MN: Bethany House, 2020), 31.

many others in this country (myself included), 9/11 came and she found herself at a crossroads. She watched as the Twin Towers smoked, as they crumbled to ash. She listened as Peter Jennings, Dan Rather, and others covered the story around the clock. And as she watched, she realized her dream. She wanted to be an on-air reporter. In fact, it's what she'd always wanted. And though her fear had immobilized her after she left college, she would not let it hold her back any longer.

It didn't take long to put things in motion. She took a job as a production assistant at a Fox and NBC dual affiliate in Dayton. A glorified go-fer, Paula wrote news copy, ran the teleprompter, brought coffee to the news anchors. On her off time, though, she took risks. She borrowed production equipment—cameras, tripods, mics—traveled to local football games, and filmed impromptu reports. She shared those reports with her producer, who laughed, saying she'd never make it on air. Undaunted, pushing the fear aside, she kept honing her skills. And then, months into chasing her dream, her producer came to her and gave her the good news. She was going on the air.

What started as field reporting for the sports department led to a co-anchor position on the sports desk. From there, Paula kept pressing, climbed the affiliate ladder to the sports desk in Cincinnati. Leaving Cincinnati, she accepted a position as a sports anchor for the ABC affiliate in Chicago, making her the first female sports anchor in a top-five broadcasting market. She could have stopped there and claimed an amazing career, but she didn't.

In 2012, Paula moved to ABC News, where she refounded her career again. Leaving sports for good, she became an anchor for ABC's *World News Now.* There, she earned her stripes, eventually going on to become a regular contributor to *Good Morning America.* In 2014, she debuted as a co-anchor on *Good Morning America Weekend,* and in 2015, she joined as a co-host on *The View* (that's right; she held her own with Whoopi Goldberg). In 2018, she became a senior national correspondent with ABC News and launched a podcast for the network. By all measures, Paula was reaping the rewards of refounding her career again and again.

Paula Faris didn't like the shape of her life while she was selling radio spots. She had the skills she needed, and the people around her believed in her. But fear held her back, crippled her. In fact, she wrote, "Fear is a liar, a dream-slayer. Fear will end your vocation before it even begins." Her solution? "[Fear] must be rooted out, even if it requires an audacious step."[29]

Born with the natural gifts and desire to enter broadcast journalism, gifted with the education to pursue her passion, the fear had nevertheless gotten the best of Paula at an early age. But when she had her own epiphany—watching the coverage of 9/11—she decided her life was worth refounding. She made a bold move, took an audacious step, and as a result, she enjoyed a successful career. But did she stop there? Hardly.

I spoke with Paula during the writing of this book, and she shared some big news. Despite having reached the pinnacle of success, she was stepping down. She would continue to use her journalism skills in unique ways. She was host to the Global Leadership Summit, a two-day leadership event held in the Chicago area, and was continuing to curate her podcast. She

---

29. Ibid., 65.

was exploring ways to celebrate women, too, and was busy planning a new business venture aimed at doing just that. She had sensed a new calling setting in, but to follow it, she'd have to refound her life.

I asked whether any of that old fear haunted her as she considers this new opportunity. She didn't miss a beat. "There should be no regrets in taking risks," she said. "If I look back on my life, when I've stepped into fear even when it didn't make sense to pivot, good things happened. Now, I don't go into something new thinking, 'What's the worst that can happen?' but 'What's the best thing that can happen?'"

Paula has taken a Refounder's approach. She examined her vocational trajectory, matched it up against her life calling, and decided it was time to refound her career. And though refounding meant change and uncertainty, though it could be a fearful experience for many, she didn't allow the fear to get in her way. She made the move. The result? Time will tell, but if you ask, she'll tell you she's happier and more at peace than she's ever been. If you ask her, she'll tell you she's already reaping the rewards.

REFOUNDERS RULES FOR REAPING REWARDS

The rewards of meaningful work—isn't that the dream?

As I write this book, the little company we refounded serves nearly 20,000 facilities across the country and has a compound annual growth rate of more than 35 percent for 20 consecutive years. We were continuing to grow and were backed by one of the largest private equity firms in the world. We've been a nine-time honoree of *Inc. Magazine*'s fastest-growing companies and have been named one of *Becker's Healthcare's* Top Places to Work and *Modern Healthcare's* Best Places to Work. Our teammates are regularly recognized as experts in their fields. Still, these aren't the things that motivate us. Instead, we focus on different rewards—the patients we impact daily, our client engagement, and the culture of engagement experienced by our people.

Paula Faris measures the rewards of her Refounding in less tangible ways, too. She may not be seen by millions of viewers, may not be climbing the corporate ladder to the bigger, better media job. Still, as she pursues the things she's passionate about—faith, leadership, and serving women—she's finding renewed joy, peace, and a renewed sense of purpose. And she's having fun doing it.

Refounders reap rewards. Sometimes those rewards are tangible—profits, growth, achieving key performance indicators. Sometimes the rewards are less tangible—the renewal of culture, more focused purpose, increased connection in your neighborhood, the joy that comes from doing something you love. But how do you stay the course of refounding so that you can reap its rewards? Consider these Refounder's Rules for Reaping Rewards:

1. TAKE A SOBER LOOK: RECOGNIZE AND PUSH BACK THE FEAR

When Chris and I began the refounding, we were barely out of college and had little in the way of real-world business experience. We'd never negotiated a lease, much less a mountain of debt. We didn't have a clear product. To say there was fear at the prospect of refounding would be an understatement.

Truth be told, the fear of failure was a massive motivator.

In the same way, Paula Faris wrestled through her own fears over the years. She'd struggled with self-doubt, with the voices that told her she wasn't good enough. But after the attacks of 9/11, she woke up to the fact that fear was keeping her from her dreams. Recognizing that fear, she stepped right into the middle of it. She took whatever job she could and made the most of it. Step by step, she worked her way from Dayton to New York City. Still, when it came time for her to leave ABC News, she could have allowed the voices to keep her from making the jump. She could have permitted the fear of what others thought to influence her decision. She didn't, though. She took the jump.

In our VUCA(R) world, we need Refounders who are willing to rebuild what's broken. Too often, though, fear keeps us from digging in and doing the hard thing. The fear may come through external circumstances—a difficult Problem Zero, shareholder expectations (remember our proxy fight in chapter 7?), or even potential workplace harassment. The fear might be stoked by our own inner demons, too—the quiet voice that tells us we're not good enough, smart enough, or even extroverted enough. To reap the rewards of refounding, though, you must be willing to push through the fear and do the hard thing.

You don't have to push through the fear alone, however. Find a mentor or an executive coach, perhaps someone like Anthony. If you're plagued by inner fear, consider seeing a therapist or counselor. Develop a personal board of directors. Surround yourself with people who will help you see past the fear and step into a Refounder's role with clarity and determination.

2. REFOUNDER'S FOCUS: REFOUNDERS DON'T LOSE SIGHT OF PEOPLE

Throughout this book, I've admonished you to focus, focus, focus on the task at hand. In the process of focusing—whether on the product offerings, on your bigger purpose, or on reinvesting in yourself—there will be times when you need to kill your darlings. But please know this: Killing your darlings does not mean killing your friends, family members, or teammates (either metaphorically or literally). What do I mean?

As Refounders, everything we do is oriented to creating better realities for humans. That being the case, you cannot refound at the expense of the humans in your organization, community, or family. More simply put, you have to remember that you are not alone.

You may be in a large corporation or in an organization with a handful of people. You might be like John Wallace, hoping to refound a neighborhood with a group of like-minded community members. Even if you're refounding your life trajectory, chances are, a spouse or a few children will be forced to take the Refounder's ride with you.

Don't leave them in the dust. Don't kill these darlings.

The Refounder's journey will not just impact your life. It will impact the lives of those in your company, community, or family. So, make sure you focus on your coworkers, neighbors, and family members. Listen to them. Take their input. Refine your direction based on their ideas, expectations, and needs. Invite them into the bigger purpose. And if you do it right, you'll see how reaping the rewards of refounding is more enjoyable with a team. You'll see how refounding creates better outcomes for everyone.

3. IMAGINING NEW POSSIBILITIES: KEEP YOUR EYES ON THE REWARD

In any refounding process, the potential rewards are just that—potential. Refounders don't lose sight of the potential. They imagine those potential outcomes as possibilities. They orient their efforts around those imagined rewards.

Consider the ultimate reward of your refounding effort. Consider the potential benefit to society, the potential cultural payoffs, and the potential profit of a successful refounding effort. Write those imagined outcomes in a journal, on a notecard, or somewhere where you'll review them regularly. Then, chase them relentlessly.

4. CREATING BETTER REALITIES: MEASURE THE ROI (THE RETURN ON INTANGIBLES)

Refounders may need to focus only on the balance sheet for a season. They may need to crunch numbers regularly. But true Refounders see beyond the profit-loss statement and pursue more meaningful, human-forward values. These values may be intangible assets, but they bring clarity of purpose and infuse the refounding process with human-focused meaning.

When businesses align with human-forward values, they experience better outcomes. They're more responsive to their customers, more caring toward their employees, and more generous to their community. They do things aligned with the bigger purpose. Aligning with these intangibles cements your identity, brings more joy and fulfillment in what you do. And though it's hard to measure joy and fulfillment, aligning your action with your intangible bigger purpose ultimately produces more measurable rewards—a better bottom line, higher employee engagement, a cleaner community.

Push through the fear, recognize others, imagine the rewards, and measure the return on intangibles as you go. If you do these things consistently, you'll begin to see the kinds of returns that strengthen your refounding resolve. You'll double down on your bigger purposes, and you'll see the exponential effect of those efforts.

We doubled down on our bigger purpose, putting human flourishing at the center of our business—flourishing for the patient, employee, and shareholder. As a result, we reaped incredible rewards. Some of those rewards were more tangible—corporate growth, private equity investment, larger shareholder returns. Many of those rewards were less measurable, though just as real—an incredible corporate culture, a place where work was a joy instead of drudgery. And so long as we keep focused on those bigger purposes, I believe we'll continue to reap the rewards. I believe you will, too.

REFOUNDER TAKEAWAYS

- Refounders push back the fear in order to pursue meaningful, purpose-filled work.
- Refounders celebrate and encourage the people who advance meaningful, purpose-filled work.
- Refounders align with human-forward values, which allows them to experience better, more meaningful outcomes.

ELEVEN

REMAINING A REFOUNDER

Successful Refounders aren't made overnight. They may have certain inclinations and motivational patterns, but most develop over time. And though I certainly developed a Refounder's mentality over the years, the truth is, I've always had a sort of rebellious streak, one that often runs through Refounders.

My college experience was not unusual. After my senior year at Central Catholic High School, nestled between CMU and the University of Pittsburgh, I left the comfort of my home and landed on the campus of a small liberal arts university located in the rolling hills somewhere in the Midwest. It was a beautiful campus, full of green space and mature trees, and it had a crystalline pond in the center of campus. But as beautiful as the campus was, my dorm room was quite the opposite. It was a simple box with two beds and spartan, Soviet-era closets. The cinder-block walls were coated with too many layers of cream-colored paint, and standing in that room, I was completely uninspired. In fact, it felt like a tan prison.

I'd received a copy of the dorm rules upon check-in, and so I pored over the pages. There were check-in and check-out policies. There were policies for quiet hours. And buried in the back was a single sentence about property destruction. To the best of my memory, it read, "for each wall that needs repainting, a $50 fee will apply upon check-out."

I set my sights on the largest wall opposite the closets. It measured seventeen feet long, a perfect blank canvas. Aside from the repainting fee, were there any rules against throwing a different coat of paint on it? I paused. Read it again. I'd read it right. I could do anything I wanted to the walls for a fifty-dollar repainting charge. And even then, the penalty wouldn't kick in until I checked out, nine months later.

Game on.

That afternoon, I made my way to a local paint store and purchased four cans of spray paint. I used tape to outline a giant mural, something that approximated street art. When I was satisfied with the outlines, I shut the door, opened the windows, and popped the tops on the spray paint cans. A few hours and a lot of fumes later, I stood back and surveyed my work. It wasn't a Banksy, but to say my environment was more interesting would be an understatement. For the price of spray paint and a deferred payment of fifty bucks, I'd created the kind of place where I could enjoy spending the next nine months.

Word got out. Other students dropped in to see my mural. The resident assistants were astounded. My room became a sort of dorm lounge, a gathering place for people who needed breaks from their own dull environments.

You might argue that my act was less of a refounding effort and more of a redecorating effort. Fair enough. But as I've written this book, events like this kept coming to mind. Why? Because, it was the first time I recall working through the entire chain of Refounder steps. I noticed something broken (the aesthetic context in the dorm room) and set out to make it more vibrant (at least to an eighteen-year-old college freshman). I took a sober look at my dorm room wall, eliminated several viable options, imagined a new possibility, and set out to create better realities for my roommate, those on my floor, and ultimately, for me.

As I've argued throughout this book, Refounders take a fundamentally different approach to rebuilding anything that's broken. They explore viable angles, learn the rules of the environment, and adapt to that learning. Put another way, they seek to become masters of the context, and then they act based on that context. And if there's one man who understands just how important contextual mastery is to refounding efforts, it's Dr. Joshua Margolis.

CONTEXTUAL LEADERSHIP IN AN EVOLVING WORLD

Psychological research shows that each of us has a unique way of coping with both personal and professional adversity. Some cut and run. Some can't let go of the past and try to hold on to the status quo. Some reimagine and fight to change the status quo. In their *Harvard Business Review* article, "How to Bounce Back from Adversity," Joshua Margolis and Paul Stoltz stated,

> Resilient managers move quickly from analysis
> to a plan of action (and reaction). After the onset
> of adversity, they shift from cause-oriented
> thinking to response-oriented thinking, and
> their focus is strictly forward.[30]

In other words, resilient managers might ask, "What happened?" but they do not dwell on the answer. Instead, they turn to go-forward thinking. Resilient managers imagine what could be and how to get to that possibility. While the past has its importance and place, Refounders are working with intention toward a better future.

Dr. Margolis is an accomplished professor at Harvard Business School in the field of leadership and ethics. According to his bio, he "is an expert in complex situations involving tradeoffs. In particular, he focuses on the distinctive ethical challenges that arise in organizations and how managers can navigate perform-or-else settings."

Over the course of several conversations, he shared his thoughts about great business leaders, including great Refounders. He starts with a foundational truth. Any successful business endeavor, whether founding or refounding, requires a sort of singularly minded focus, a fierce conviction. Still, he says, there's a difference between having a fierce conviction and being closed-minded. Business leaders must be both convicted and open-minded. They must continue to employ a learner's mindset in everything they do, particularly

---

30. Joshua Margolis and Paul Stoltz, "How to Bounce Back from Adversity," *Harvard Business Review* (January–February 2010), https://hbr.org/2010/01/how-to-bounce-back-from-adversity (accessed November 21, 2020).

as the facts and circumstances of the world change.

But what is a learner's mentality?

Learners, he says, don't pursue static courses. They assimilate information, learn, and adjust to that information. What's more, they create minimum viable products (MVPs as many in software development call them) that allow them to reduce ideas to a concrete product. They use that product to test their assumptions and then ask, *What has to be true in the world to make it work?*

Sounds familiar, doesn't it?

This is what we did with our initial wound tracking system.

This is what John Wallace did in Homewood.

This is what Astro Teller does at X.

The learner's approach—the approach of testing assumptions, gathering data, and responding—is more important than ever, Margolis says. I don't need to ask what he means, but he tells me anyway. We're in the middle of what he calls a "pandemic winter," a season where the rules are changing rapidly. Assumptions are being undermined. What used to work doesn't anymore.

Recalling the early months of the pandemic, Dr. Margolis notes that there was a sort of excitement in the air when COVID-19 made landfall in the United States. People stockpiled and hunkered down. They thought they could wait it out. But as the pandemic winter dragged on, as lockdowns set in and the rug got pulled out from under the economy, a new reality set in. The world was drastically different.

I knew this to be true. Jen and I hadn't taken an honest date in months. All of our favorite coffee shops, cafes, and restaurants were closed. Some grocery stores were experiencing food shortages. Everyone who could work from home was required to. This was a massive disrupter of culture.

Yes, the world was in need of new models. But how could we do that if we weren't open to learning from the changing context? As if intuiting my question, Margolis asks, "What is the work of leadership and management as we come out of this winter? Leaders need to be equipped to not have the answers. They must be equipped to deal with the challenges the likes of which they've never encountered."

It's a weighty statement.

He continues, sharing that this should be the primary function of graduate business schools in the future. Nuts and bolts are still important—the basic languages and skill sets of finance, economics, accounting, and management—but future leaders must learn to assimilate information in unexpected circumstances, learn from it, and act on it. In other words, the leaders of the future—including Refounders—will do their best to become masters of their own context.

Contextual intelligence is the key to navigating the many crises of the future, Dr. Margolis said. And so, contextual intelligence is the key for any refounding effort.

CREATING A REFOUNDER'S WORKING PLAN

As we've seen throughout this book, masters of refounding share certain skills. They're able to stop and take a sober look at their surroundings. They focus on what's really important, and as they do, they imagine new and better possibilities. Then, they get to work, creating better worlds for the people around them. But as I look to all the Refounders I wrote about in this book—and the many Refounders I didn't include—there's another commonality. Refounders are masters of their context, and they operate with a learner's mentality.

What do I mean?

Refounders take the time to understand the world around them. They recognize crisis moments. They seek information from experts when necessary and allow that information to shape their decision making. They know their organizations, neighborhoods, and industries, too. They see how those systems react to volatility in the world around them. They devote themselves to understanding the context of the world so they can be effective Refounders.

If I've heard it once, I've heard it a thousand times: Context matters. This aphorism is especially true as a Refounder. So as you go about your own refounding efforts, take the time to stop and learn. Take a look at the changes in the world around you and learn how those changes impact your business, neighborhood, or family. Examine your failures and learn from them. Understand how market conditions have undermined your assumptions and derailed your progress. Learn, learn, learn everything you can about your context. Then, with a fuller understanding, begin the refounding process.

When we began our corporate turnaround, we hadn't identified the key steps to refounding: Take a sober look; develop a Refounder's focus; imagine new possibilities; and create better realities for humans. What's more, though we might have intuited it, we didn't set out to master our context with any sort of intentional focus. Simply put, we sort of stumbled our way through the refounding and learned the lessons along the way. But the truth is, looking back, I see that many of the skills I used in the refounding process were honed much earlier in my life. Seeing what's broken, imagining better possibilities, using contextual learning—I'd exhibited all of those characteristics when I repainted my dorm. And the truth is, if you look back at some event in your life, you'll likely see that you've exhibited similar skills at one point or another. How do I know? Because humans are Refounders at heart.

Because you picked up this book, because you made it all the way to the final chapter, there's a good chance you're in or near a refounding season. Things might seem broken in your company, neighborhood, community of faith, or marriage. Maybe your corporate division isn't as profitable as it needs to be or the creative team is no longer making magic. Maybe your neighborhood is in decline or your block needs beautification. Perhaps your work lacks meaning because your team is not focused on a bigger purpose. Maybe your work culture feels akin to a prison sentence. You could cut and run, and on some days, that might be tempting. And some situations may merit an exit. But before you do, stop and ask yourself: What would a Refounder do?

- A Refounder would take a sober look at what's broken.
- A Refounder would determine the Problem Zero.
- A Refounder would focus by killing their darlings.
- A Refounder would imagine new possibilities.
- A Refounder would work to create better realities for people.
- A Refounder would do it all using contextual learning as their guide.

I'm fortunate to have played a part in a refounding. Without walking through the crisis and into resolution, I wouldn't have the same worldview. It has shaped the way I think, the way I work, and the companies I invest in and consult with. I wouldn't have been surrounded by amazing people like Anthony, Chris, and so many others. I wouldn't have known exactly how much a band of committed Refounders was capable of—because it really does take a team. And remember the part we played in helping Caryl during the pandemic? That, too, never would have happened.

All of us have a part to play in refounding some part of the world. We've each been gifted a unique opportunity to take something broken and make it better, continuously. If I didn't believe this was true, I wouldn't be writing this book.

Have you identified the place where you are called to refound? As you've read, have you had a nudge or an inkling about the thing that's broken that only you can make better? If so, great. Get on it. Work the plan. But if you haven't, carve out an hour over the next week and ask yourself: *What feels broken in my business, my community, or my personal life that I can make better?* And once you determine the area you've been called to refound, write it down in a notebook, laptop, tablet, or on a notecard. Keep it somewhere where you will see it regularly. Then, set out to create a Refounder's Working Plan. Write down each of the four steps: taking a sober look; developing a Refounder's focus; imagining new possibilities; and creating better realities for the people in your life. Leave space after each step to brainstorm your own refounding path.

Return to your Refounder's Working Plan regularly. Modify it as you learn, as the context changes. And if you fail from time to time in the process, don't give up. Call in experts if needed. Call in veteran Refounders. Whatever you do, keep working the plan.

Remember: successful refounding is not a one-and-done process. It is an ongoing process that takes a certain mentality, an ongoing way of being. Cultivate that mentality. Put it into action. Then, go. Become a Refounder.

REFOUNDER TAKEAWAYS

- Refounders become masters of context, taking in as much information about their environments to rebuild businesses, systems, structures, or practices that thrive.
- Refounders know they don't have all the answers, but they work tirelessly to imagine and implement solutions to emerging and complex problems.
- Refounding is an ongoing process, and true Refounders cultivate the mentality and practices to engage in that process for a lifetime.

ACKNOWLEDGMENTS

To my friends, family, and teammates who helped brew the creative coffee that made this story true.

To Christopher Hayes and Anthony Sanzo, my partners.

To Don, John, and Dave for getting this band started in your garage so many years ago.

To Erika Nicholson and Josh Moyer, true creatives.

To the remarkable Seth Haines, the sober "kyd" that helped imagine better possibilities for all people. Your creativity, wit, and turn-of-a-phrase have made all the difference.

To my mother for proofing, improving, and being living proof.

To Brian Turk, Steve Fleck, and Jason Wolfe for friendship and candid feedback.

To Dr. David Armstrong Bill Flanaghan, Dr. Karon Cook, Dr. Foluso Fakorede, Paula Faris, Dr. Chris Howard, Heidi Jannenga, Joshua Margolis, Audrey Russo, Lisa Slayton, Astro Teller, and Jessica Trybus.

To advisors past and present: Steve Bailey, Brent Burns, Patrick Cline, Mike Gozycki, Jeff Haywood, Jim Jordan, Ruben King-Shaw, Ben Levin, Donna Morea, Charlie Munzig, Jim Quagliaroli, and Bill Winkenwerder.

To my teammates: Josh Pickus, Christine Jones, Linda Kricher, Jason Baim, Aaron Brandwein, Jason James, and the one and only, Patrick Rooney.

Finally, my longstanding gratitude to the 1,000+ colleagues and 200,000+ caregivers connected to Net Health. You made our transformation from broken to better possible.

ABOUT THE AUTHOR

PATRICK COLLETTI is a Refounder. As the President of Net Health for two decades, he and his partners led the organization from the brink of bankruptcy to a healthcare technology company that helps caregivers heal millions of people each year while consistently being ranked locally and nationally for its award winning culture. An experienced board director and advisor for angel, VC, and PE backed organizations, Colletti is a frequent speaker, selective consultant, and redemptive investor. Drawing on his executive experience, business-growth expertise, and passion for creating humanity-enriching corporate culture, Patrick teaches corporate and community leaders how to take a hard look at what's broken, imagine new possibilities, and work toward creating better realities. This is the work of a Refounder.

He is the recipient of the Ernst and Young Entrepreneur of the Year Award and lives in Pittsburgh with his wife, Jennifer, and sons, Hudson and Andrew.

r